ARTIFICIAL INTELLIGENCE
AND
HUMAN COGNITION

ARTIFICIAL INTELLIGENCE

—— AND ——

HUMAN COGNITION

A THEORETICAL INTERCOMPARISON OF TWO REALMS OF INTELLECT

MORTON WAGMAN

PRAEGER

New York
Westport, Connecticut
London

Library of Congress Cataloging-in-Publication Data

Wagman, Morton.
    Artificial intelligence and human cognition: a theoretical
intercomparison of two realms of intellect / Morton Wagman.
        p.   cm.
    Includes bibliographical references and indexes.
    ISBN 0-275-93615-5
    1. Cognition—Data processing.   2. Artificial intelligence.
3. Cognitive science.   I. Title.
    BF311.W2659   1991
    153.4—dc20   90-42682

British Library Cataloguing in Publication Data is available.

Library of Congress Catalog Card Number: 90-42682
ISBN: 0-275-93615-5

First published in 1991

Praeger Publishers, One Madison Avenue, New York, NY 10010
An imprint of Greenwood Publishing Group, Inc.

Printed in the United States of America

The paper used in this book complies with the
Permanent Paper Standard issued by the National
Information Standards Organization (Z39.48-1984).

10 9 8 7 6 5 4 3 2 1

Contents

Contents

Tables and Figures

TABLES

FIGURES

Preface

This book examines the emulation of human cognition by artificial intelligence systems. Human thought and computer thought are compared in their distinctiveness and commonality.

Chapter 1 presents a general introduction to the computational modelling of cognition. The nature and significance of the production system formalism in cognitive science theory is discussed.

Computational reasoning and human rationality are considered in Chapter 2. Computational reasoning is exemplified by the intellectual contribution of sophisticated systems to the establishment of mathematical proof and by the demonstration competence of an advanced system for the careful discernment of legal issues in contract law.

The range, depth, and sensitivity of these mathematical and legal reasoning systems are compared with human mathematicians and human jurisprudence. General issues concerning the quality of human rationality are examined in several contexts: the prediction of economic behavior, mathematical abstraction and the concept of the infinitesimal, and probabilistic judgment under uncertainty.

The nature of problem solving in the context of general intellectual principles and specific domain knowledge is examined in Chapter 3. The ability of the FERMI (Flexible Expert Reasoner with Multi-domain Inferencing) system to deploy the general strategies of decomposition and invariance across several domains of physical science is described. Limitations on the applied flexibility and theoretical depth of the FERMI system are contrasted with human creativity. In the second part of the chapter, the cognitive processes that distinguish expert from inexpert cardiologists in the establishment of the valid differential diagnosis of endocarditis are analyzed in terms of differential hierarchies of production rules embodying specialized knowledge.

Chapter 4 is concerned with the cognition of scientific discovery. In the first part of the chapter, the *Kekada* program is described. *Kekada* constitutes a close simulation of the specific patterns of experimental investigation that characterize an important discovery in biochemistry. The potential usefulness of KEKADA as a general model of scientific discovery processes is analyzed. In the second part of the chapter, the processes of scientific discovery are examined in a laboratory context. Theoretical and experimental modes of scientific discovery are identified and explicated in a hierarchical model of scientific discovery as a dual search in a hypothesis space and an experiment space. The model is contrasted with accounts of scientific discovery and with theories of creative insight and problem representation.

Language representation modes and information-processing efficiency are discussed in Chapter 5. Sentential representation and diagrammatic representation of the same information have differential effects on the efficiency of information processing. A formal explanation of the strategic advantage of diagrammatic representation in certain types of problem solving is given. A discussion of how diagrammatic representation may limit the scope of mathematical thought is also presented.

In the concluding chapter, the most impressive intellectual achievements of artificial intelligence systems considered in this book are summarized, and directions for further intellectual advancement in this area are indicated.

The volume is intended for graduate and advanced undergraduate students in cognitive science programs, psychology, philosophy, and artificial intelligence courses, and for professionals in these and related disciplines.

The book's provision of both detailed examples of artificial intelligence programs that accomplish highly intellectual tasks and of general theoretical perspectives on the nature of cognition will enable it to be used as a source and a stimulus by all, both students and professionals, who are curious about the human mind and the extent to which it is a mechanism that can be emulated by the mechanisms of artificial intelligence.

I am grateful to Betty Jang and Catherine Laine for their excellent typing of the manuscript. I am also grateful to LaDonna Wilson for her assistance in the preparation of the tables and figures and for proofreading.

ONE

Introduction

It is not my aim to surprise or shock you . . . . But the simplest way I can summarize is to say that there are now in the world machines that think, that learn, and that create. Moreover, the ability to do these things is going to increase rapidly until — in a visible future — the range of problems they can handle will be co-extensive with the range to which the human mind has been applied.

H.A. Simon, in McCorduck, 1979, p. 188

PSYCHOLOGY AND ARTIFICIAL INTELLIGENCE

Contemporary psychology, in broad outline, is dominated by three general viewpoints or theories: evolutionary theory, psychoanalytic theory, and computational theory.

In evolutionary theory, the environment reinforces certain behaviors of the organism, resulting in survival. Behavior that is reinforced is adjustive and adaptive to the environment.

In psychoanalytic theory, adaptation and adjustment result from the harmonious integration of dynamic aspects of the personality. Conflicts between motives and values result in anxiety. Defense mechanisms control anxiety, but at the cost of producing rigidity and neurosis in the personality.

In computational theory, the mind is viewed as mechanism. The mechanisms of human thought can be described mathematically. Reasoning is but reckoning. Problem solving is but calculating.

The computational theory of psychology finds its model in artificial intelligence, the science that holds that computers, by virtue of their mathematical structure, can reason. Artificial intelligence does not require the computer to understand what it is reasoning about.

The reasoning mechanism is a calculus indifferent to its content. In contrast, the calculus of human thought is, as demonstrated in the psychoanalytic theory of psychology, distinctly responsive to the content and import of personal ideation. Thus, at most, artificial intelligence can model only the mechanics of human reasoning and human problem solving.

The mathematical descriptions of human thought and computer thought may approach an identical form. Such a universal mathematical description of reasoning and problem solving can be valuable for both human psychology and artificial intelligence. Advances in knowledge of the mechanisms of thought in one domain benefit the other domain as well.

Just as mathematical description is a language expressing the essentiality of relationships between theoretical variables, so symbolic logic in the language of the propositional and predicate calculus expresses the essentiality of the structure or architecture of thought; and just as mathematical symbols can be manipulated instead of manipulating physical reality, so the logical calculus can be manipulated instead of manipulating cognitive reality. The language of mathematics is to physical reality as the language of the predicate calculus is to cognitive reality.

The mapping of cognitive reality in a general programming language that would accommodate the general structure or architecture of thought has been attempted by a number of cognitive scientists. An important example of John Anderson's unitary theory of cognition:

I would like to head off two possible misinterpretations of my position. First, the unitary position is not incompatible with the fact there are distinct systems for vision, audition, walking, and so on. My claim is only that higher-level cognition involves a unitary system. Of course, the exact boundaries of higher-level cognition are a little uncertain, but its contents are not trivial; language, mathematics, reasoning, memory, and problem solving should certainly be included. Second, the unitary position should not be confused with the belief that the human mind is simple and can be explained by just one or two principles. An appropriate analogy would be to a programming language like INTERLISP (Teitleman, 1976), which is far from simple and which supports a great variety of data structures and functions. However, it is *general-purpose,* that is, one can use the same data structures and processes in programs for language and for problem solving. Individual programs can be created that do language and problem solving as special cases. In analogy to INTERLISP, I claim that a single set of principles underlies all of cognition and that there are no principled differences or separations of faculties. It is in this sense that the theory is unitary. (Anderson, 1983, p. 5)

A different, more abstract, and inclusive *general unified theory of intelligence* can be formulated on the basis of the logic of implication. This *fundamental theorem of intelligence* would hold that the logic of implication (if *p,* then *q*) subsumes both the formal structure of human reasoning and problem solving and the formal structure of artificial intelligence. The logic of implication is foundational to mathematical and scientific reasoning and to the reasoning of everyday behavior as well (Wagman, 1978, 1984a), and is foundational to programming logic and knowledge representation formalisms in artificial intelligence systems (Wagman, 1980, 1988, in press).

The principal mechanism for problem solving in artificial intelligence is the production system (Hunt, 1989; Nilsson, 1980; Rolston, 1988). The production system has its conceptual source in the mathematical logic of E. L. Post (1943) and its derived application in the information processing theory of A. Newell and H. A. Simon (1972).

The production system was one of those happy events, though in minor key, that historians of science often talk about: a rather well-prepared formalism, sitting in wait for a scientific mission. Production systems have a long and diverse history. Their use of symbolic logic starts with Post (1943), from whom the name is taken. They also show up as Markov algorithms (1954). Their use in linguistics, where they are also called rewrite rules, dates from Chomsky (1957). As with so many other notions in computer science, they really entered into wide currency when they became operationalised in programming languages. (Newell and Simon, 1972, p. 889).

The production system consists of three modular elements: a global data base, a set of production rules, and a set of control structures. The modularity of the elements allows for their modification without any complicating interaction effects. The content of the elements consists of encoded knowledge in a given problem domain. Production rules are composed of condition–action pairs. Satisfaction by the data base of the conditions of production rules instigates their operation. The determination of the specific sequence of production rules in a cycle of operations is a major function of the control structures.

In applying production systems to problem solving, pathways through the problem space (the set of possible problem states) are searched until the goal state is achieved. The sequence of operations of the production system directs a search trajectory. Trajectories are mapped onto a search tree structure consisting of nodes that represent problem states and directed arcs that represent production rules. Search tree structures developed in the course of solving problems in legal reasoning can be found in Chapter 2 (Figure 2.6).

In Chapter 4, the scope of application of production rule methodology is enlarged in order to provide for a computational model of the processes of scientific discovery. The model includes heuristic production rules for generating search trajectories through a hypothesis space and an experiment space. The model, KEKADA, successfully emulates the cognitive processes and scientific discoveries of the eminent biochemist, Hans Krebs.

The emulation of cognitive processes by artificial intelligence systems is a major theme of this book. Systematic comparisons of similarity and contrast between human thought and computer thought are drawn, and the distinctive qualities of intellectual performance that characterize each mode of cognition are examined in depth.

TWO

Reasoning and Rationality

In the first section of this chapter, the intellectual contributions of artificial intelligence to mathematical reasoning are exemplified by the problem of proving the four-color conjecture. The establishment of this proof had eluded the best mathematicians for over a century, and required the acceptance of the computer as a genuine contributor to mathematical reasoning. The section concludes with a comparison of mathematical theorem proving by mathematicians and by computers.

In the second section of the chapter, the general logic of computer jurisprudence is discussed. An artificial intelligence approach to legal reasoning is exemplified by the Gardner Legal Reasoning Program. The reasoning of the program is compared with the reasoning of Harvard Law School students in response to a problem in contract law. The program correctly discerned a larger number of legal issues in the problem than did the students. The section concludes with a comparison of computer jurisprudence and human jurisprudence.

In the third section of the chapter, the rationality of human cognition is examined. Limitations on the rationality of theories in economics are discussed. The rationality of mathematics is considered with reference to abstraction and idealization, the nature of non-Euclidean geometry, and the concept of the infinitesimal. The rationality of everyday behavior is examined in the context of psychological research on probabilistic reasoning. The section concludes with a commentary on the problem of establishing criteria for the definition and evaluation of human rationality.

ARTIFICIAL INTELLIGENCE AND MATHEMATICAL REASONING

The Four-Color Problem and Its Computer-Dependent Solution

From the time of Euclid's proof of the Pythagorean Theorem, the proof of theorems in all areas of mathematics (algebra, analysis, and topology) has resulted from the rigorous methods of human mathematicians (Boyer, 1968). Proofs of mathematical conjectures could be checked for their validity by careful examination of the completeness and precision of the proofs' rationality (Hardy, 1929). It was, therefore, a dramatic change in the methods of mathematical proof and mathematical discovery (Polya, 1962) when Kenneth Appel and Wolfgang Haken (1977, 1979) developed a mathematical proof of the four-color conjecture that was absolutely dependent on computer rationality and could be checked for validity only by other independent computer programs. The proof of the four-color theorem had eluded the best efforts of human mathematicians in the century preceding the application of artificial intelligence to the problem. In this section, the nature of the four-color problem, mathematical methods proposed for its solution, Appel and Haken's computer-dependent proof, and the implication of this new mode of mathematical rationality will be discussed.

The Nature of the Four-Color Problem

From the ease with which the four-color conjecture is stated, it might appear that a proof of its truth or falsity could be readily established. Originally posed by Francis Gurthrie in 1852, the four-color conjecture states that four colors are sufficient to color every map so that neighboring countries sharing a common border have different colors. The basic ideas for proving the conjecture were developed in 1878 by Arthur Kempe. Kempe's ideas included the concept of a normal map, a proported proof based on reductio ad absurdum argument, and the method of unavoidable sets and reducible configurations.

Along with the extracts by Appel and Haken (1979), Figure 2.1 presents the important ideas concerning normal maps, and Figure 2.2 presents an explanation of Kempe's incomplete reductio ad absurdum proof of the four-color conjecture.

Figure 2.1
Normal Maps

Source: K. Appel and W. Haken; The Four-Color Problem (in L. A. Steen, ed., *Mathematics Today: Twelve Informal Essays,* New York: Springer-Verlag, 1979), p. 158–159.

A normal map is one in which no more than three regions meet at any point, and in which no region entirely encircles another one. The states in the eastern half of the United States form a normal map, but the entire continental United States does not – because Utah, Nevada, Arizona and New Mexico all meet at a single point. Since every map can be associated with a normal map which requires at least as many colors, it is sufficient to prove the Four-Color Conjecture for normal maps, for if it is true for these maps then it will be true for all maps. One then shows that any normal map (in a plane) satisfies the formula

$$4p_2 + 3p_3 + 2p_4 + p_5 - p_7 - 2p_8 - 3p_9 - \cdots - (-6)p_n = 12$$

where p_n is the number of countries of the map that have exactly n neighbors and N is the largest number of neighbors that any country has. (Note that n = 0 and n = 1 cannot occur in a normal map since no enclaves or islands can occur in normal maps; thus the formula begins with p_2.) Now each p_n is either positive or zero and occurs in the formula with a positive sign only if n is less than 6. Thus for the formula to have a positive sum on the left (to match the positive number on the right) at least one of p_2, p_3, p_4, or p_5 must be positive. In other words, some country must have either two, three, four, or five neighbors. (Appel and Haken, 1979, pp. 158–159)

Figure 2.2
Kempe's Proported Proof of the Four-Color Conjecture

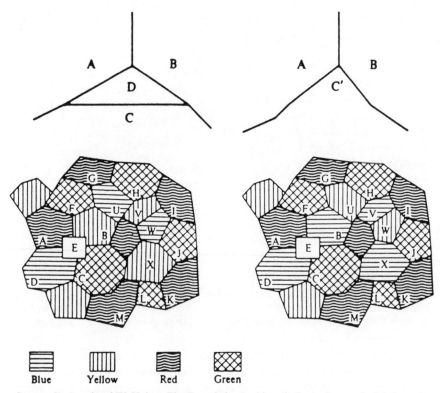

Blue   Yellow   Red   Green

Source: K. Appel and W. Haken, The Four-Color Problem (in L. A. Steen, ed., *Mathematics Today: Twelve Informal Essays,* New York: Springer-Verlag, 1979), p. 160–161.

The crux of Kempe's proported proof of the Four-Color Conjecture is that a minimal five-chromatic normal map (a smallest normal map that requires five colors) cannot contain any country with exactly two, three, four, or five neighbors. Since Kempe knew that every normal map must contain such a country, he concluded that there is no smallest normal map requiring five colors. Hence there can't be any map that requires five colors. To outline Kempe's argument, we will examine in detail how his proof went for countries with three or four neighbors.

Suppose a minimal five-chromatic map had a country with exactly three neighbors (like country D on the left in Figure 2.2). If that country is amalgamated with one of its neighbors (as on the right in Figure 2.2, where countries C and D are united to form country C^1), then the resulting map has fewer countries than a minimal five-chromatic map. Hence it is colorable with four colors.

Now if all the countries except the amalgamated country (D) of the original map are assigned the colors of the corresponding countries in the map obtained by the amalgamation, the amalgamated country may be colored with the color not assigned to any of its three neighbors. Thus the original map must have been four-colorable, contradicting the assumption that it was five-chromatic. (Essentially the same argument suffices to show that no country in a minimal five-chromatic map can have exactly two neighbors.)

The corresponding argument for four neighbors is an idea of major importance in Kempe's work. Suppose that a minimal five-chromatic map has a country with exactly four neighbors. As before, one can amalgamate such a country and color the rest of the map with four colors, leaving the amalgamated country uncolored (as in Figure 2.2, where the country with four neighbors is E). Now if the four neighbors of the uncolored country are colored with fewer than four distinct colors, a color may be chosen for the remaining country. Otherwise, the following argument of Kempe suffices.

Consider the colors of a pair of countries on opposite sides of the uncolored country (for example, the red of country A and the green of country C). Either there is a path of adjacent countries colored with those two colors leading from one of the countries to the other, or there is not. (In the figure above, the path consisting of countries A, F, G, H, I, J, K, L, M, and C has only countries colored red and green and leads from A to C. On the other hand there is no path consisting of countries colored yellow and blue leading from B to D.) In honor of Kempe, such two-colored paths are now called Kempe chains.

If both pairs of opposing countries were joined by paths of the corresponding pairs of colors, the two paths would then have a country in common, which is certainly impossible. Thus there is some pair (B and D in our example) not joined by a Kempe chain. Choose one country (say B) of the pair and list all of the countries that are colored by one of the two selected colors (in our example there would be yellow and blue, the colors of B and D) and are joined by a (yellow-blue) path to the chosen country. (In our example, countries B, U, V, W, and X form the list.) Now interchange the colors of the countries on the list. (The figure on the right in Figure 2.2 results from the figure on the left by interchanging blue and yellow on countries B, U, V, W, and X.) Now the uncolored country has neighbors of only three colors since the list of countries whose colors were interchanged cannot include more than one (in our case, B) of the four neighboring countries. Thus the uncolored country (E) may be colored with the fourth color (yellow), again leading to a contradiction with the hypothesis that the map required five colors. (adapted from Appel and Haken, 1979, pp. 160–161)

Basic to proving the four-color conjecture is the search for an unavoidable set of reducible configurations. This was Kempe's strategy, and although the development of adequate mathematical and computer methods was to take a century, Kempe's ideas were seminal in arriving at the proof.

Normal maps (see Figure 2.1) are comprised of one or more countries, each of which has either five, four, three, or two neighbors. All normal maps must be comprised of at least one of these configurations, and the set of these necessary configurations is termed an unavoidable set (see Figure 2.3). Configurations in the set can be large and complex and, depending on the details of the configuration, they may or may not be reducible. Proving that configurations are reducible depends on the type of reasoning developed by Kempe in Figure 2.2. The difficulty of finding an unavoidable set of reducible configurations (which would constitute a proof of the four-color theorem) is indicated by the fact that, although such a set might contain thousands of configurations, during the 75 years following Kempe, mathematicians had only established the four-color theorem for maps with fewer than 36 countries.

Intellectual Contributions of the Computer to the Four-Color Proof

Appel and Haken (1977, 1979) concluded, after much work, that a proof dependent on the method of establishing an unavoidable set of reducible configurations would involve thousands of configurations of various degrees of complexity, and that only a very-high-speed computer programmed to handle certain mechanical aspects of carrying out the proof would be adequate to the task. They found, much to their surprise, that as they carried out a dialogue with the computer and cyclically improved the programs, the computer, instead of functioning as a limited automaton, increasingly became an intellectual contributor with high-quality ideas, which were sometimes better than their own.

In early 1975 we modified [the] experimental program to yield obstacle-free configurations and forced it to search for arguments that employed configurations of small ring size. The resulting runs pointed out the need for new improvements in the procedure, but also yielded a very pleasant surprise: replacing geographically good configurations by obstacle-free ones did not seem to more than double the size of the unavoidable set.

At this point the program, which had by now absorbed our ideas and improvements for two years, began to surprise us. At the beginning we would check its arguments by hand so we could always predict the course it

Figure 2.3
Kempe's Small Unavoidable Set

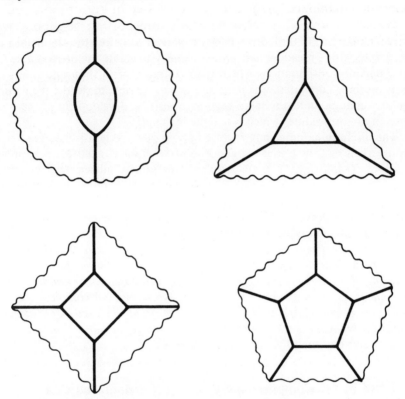

Source: Kenneth Appel and Wolfgang Haken, The Four-Color Problem (in L. A. Steen, ed., *Mathematics Today: Twelve Informal Essays,* New York: Springer-Verlag, 1979), p. 163.

would follow in any situation; but now it suddenly started to act like a chess-playing machine. It would work out compound strategies based on all the tricks it had been "taught" and often these approaches were far more clever than those we would have tried. Thus it began to teach us things about how to proceed that we never expected. In a sense it had surpassed its creators in some aspects of the "intellectual" as well as the mechanical parts of the task. (Appel and Haken, 1979, p. 175, italics added)

The Problem of Checking the Computer's Correctness by Hand

The immensity of the stream of computer and human computation that went into the proof of the four-color theorem is impressive, but as Appel and Haken indicated, checking the correctness of the computer's processing and output is not possible except with another independent computer program:

From January 1976 until June 1976 we worked to define the last details of the discharging procedure and simultaneously to create the unavoidable set of reducible configurations which it produced. Over a thousand hours of time on three computers was used and it was possible to do the reductions quickly enough (in real time) to keep pace with the development of the final discharging procedure (which was done by hand).

The discharging procedure involved about 500 special discharging situations (resulting from critical neighborhoods) that modified the first approximation of January 1976. It required analysis of about ten thousand neighborhoods of vertices of positive charge by hand and analysis of reducibility of over two thousand configurations by machine. While not all of this material became part of the final proof, a considerable part, including the proof of reducibility of about 1500 configurations, is essential. *A person could carefully check the part of the discharging procedure that did not involve reducibility computations in a month or two, but it does not seem possible to check the reducibility computations themselves by hand. Indeed, the referees of the paper resulting from our work used our complete notes to check the discharging procedure, but they resorted to an independent computer program to check the correctness of the reducibility computations.* (Appel and Haken, 1979, p. 178, italics added)

Proof by the Computer and Proof by the Mathematician

For a century before the work of Appel and Haken, mathematicians working with their customary theoretical methods had been intrigued with the simple-sounding four-color conjecture and frustrated by its resistance to proof. Appel and Haken succeeded, but only by the revolutionary step of constructing a proof constituting both computer intelligence and human intelligence. There has been resistance to this departure from the traditional methods of pure mathematics, both in mathematics and in philosophy (Tymoczko, 1979, 1980). Appel and Haken made the following interesting points:

Most mathematicians who were educated prior to the development of fast computers tend not to think of the computer as a routine tool to be used in conjunction with other older and more theoretical tools in advancing mathematical knowledge. Thus they intuitively feel that if an argument contains parts that are not verifiable by hand calculations it is on rather insecure ground. There is a tendency to feel that verification of computer results by independent computer programs is not as certain to be correct as independent hand checking of the proof of theorems proved in the standard way.

This point of view is reasonable for those theorems whose proofs are of moderate length and highly theoretical. When proofs are long and highly computational, it may be argued that even when hand checking is possible, the probability of human error is considerably higher than that of machine error; moreover, if the computations are sufficiently routine, the validity of programs themselves is easier to verify than the correctness of hand computations.

In any event, even if the Four-Color Theorem turns out to have a simpler proof, mathematicians might be well advised to consider more carefully other problems that might have solutions of this new type, requiring computation or analysis of a type not possible for humans alone. There is every reason to believe that there are a large number of such problems. After all, the argument that almost all known proofs are reasonably short can be answered by the argument that if one only employs tools which will yield short proofs that is all one is likely to get. . . . *The example of the Four-Color Theorem may help to clarify the possibilities and the limitations of the methods of pure mathematics and those of computation. It may be that a problem cannot be solved by either of these alone but can be solved by a combination of the two methods.* (Appel and Haken, 1979, pp. 178–179, italics added)

The character of the Appel and Haken proof has been judged by Thomas Tymoczko (1979, 1980), a philosopher of logic, as lacking the qualities necessary for rigorous mathematical proof of theorems. According to Tymoczko (1980), the rationality of mathematical proof must be indubitable, and proofs that are comprised, even in part, of computer computation fall short because the internal calculations and reasoning of the computer program cannot be corroborated by the human mathematical mind but only by another computer program, which is similarly limited.

If we accept the four-color theorem as a theorem, then we are committed to changing the sense of "theorem," or more to the point, to changing the sense of the underlying concept of "proof." (Thomas Tymoczko, quoted in Davis and Hersh, 1981, p. 383)

However, human reasoning in general (see the section on rationality and human cognition in this chapter), and mathematical reasoning in particular (Weissinger, 1969) — especially as it proceeds, but even in its results — cannot be guaranteed to be permanently certain and complete. Euclidean geometry as a model of mathematical

proof, after centuries of complete acceptance by students and mathematicians, was found to be incorrect (Heath, 1956) with respect to the
relationship between postulates and logical derivations (the parallel
postulate). The indubitability of the foundations of mathematics
(Fraenkel, 1947) and of the completeness of mathematical theorems
and the nature of proof (its decidability or undecidability) changed
after the work of K. Godel (Crowe, 1975; Davis, 1965; Dieudonne,
1971; Godel, 1931, 1964; Kolata, 1976; Korner, 1967; Lakatos, 1976;
Mehrtens, 1976; Rabin, 1977).

The use of computer technology, by itself, does not change the
conceptual requirements for mathematical proof (Wilder, 1944).
There is a change in method, but the objection to the employment of
computers may be a cultural lag (Tucker, 1970) or an aesthetic preference (Hardy, 1967; Wechsler, 1978), or it may represent a resistance to
a change in customary ways of thinking (Wagman, 1983).

ARTIFICIAL INTELLIGENCE AND LEGAL
REASONING

The General Logic of Computer Jurisprudence

Two objectives of artificial-intelligence legal-reasoning programs
can be distinguished: (a) out of the Gottfried Leibniz tradition, "Let
us calculate," to replace disputations of lawyers and lawyers, lawyers
and judges, or judges and judges with machine resolution of legal
problems; and (b) to model, study, and extend knowledge of human
legal reasoning, wherein the application of cognitive science might
result in an increase in the lucidity and power of legal reasoning but
human jurisprudence is not replaced by computer jurisprudence.

J. Frank (1949) provided an early description of the functions and
limitations of a possible computer jurisprudence system, and A.
Gardner (1987) implemented a system that is in general accord with
Frank's concepts. The following account by Frank provides a useful
introduction to Gardner's research:

It is conceivable that an "ultra-rapid" legal-logic machine could promptly
answer questions like these: (1) Given a specific state of facts, F, what possible alternative legal rules, R's, will logically lead to a desired decision, D? (2)
Given a legal rule, R, and a desired decision, D, what possible alternative
states of fact, F's, will logically yield that decision? (3) Given a specific legal
rule, R, and a specific state of facts, F, what is the logically correct decision, D?
Anyone who believes such a machine can supplant the human process of

judging is hoping to revert, in a scientific way, to the "mechanical" method of the ordeals. I, who have done my fair share of jeering at "mechanical jurisprudence," have no such hope. Yet I think there is much merit in the idea of such a machine. . . . [It] seems to me that judges and lawyers would benefit from having relatively simple problems — type (3) — speedily and correctly answered, and from having put before them promptly all possible alternative solutions of more complicated problems, i.e., type (1) and (2) problems. . . .

Such a machine would not reduce, but would increase, the need for legal intelligence: great skill would be necessary in formulating the questions put to the machine. Semantic difficulties would, too, in many instances, prove a stumbling block.

Moreover, even were such a machine to disclose all possible available alternative legal rules, the judges (except when bound by statute or precedents) would still have to exercise "the sovereign prerogative of choice" between the rules, on the basis of the judges' conscious or unconscious notions of policy. The machine might give judges the benefit of offering the alternatives clearly. But it would not realize the hope of Leibniz who thought that, if there were such a machine, then "If controversies were to arise, there would be no more need of disputation between two philosophers [or lawyers, we may interpolate] than between two accountants. For it would suffice [for them] . . . to say to each . . . : Let us calculate." Mr. Justice Douglas had in mind the judges' "sovereign prerogative of choice" when, in effect answering Leibniz, he said, "The law is not a series of calculating machines where . . . answers come tumbling out when the right levers are pushed." (Frank, 1949, pp. 206–208)

Gardner's Legal Reasoning Program

Gardner (1987) developed a legal reasoning system in the area of contract law. Contract law is basic in legal education and legal practice, and is one of the best defined areas of the law (American Law Institute, 1932, 1981); thus, it is most suitable for artificial intelligence approaches to the study of legal reasoning. Gardner's legal reasoning system was intended to analyze and offer an acceptance problem. The analysis would distinguish between clear aspects of the problem and complex aspects that would involve issues whose resolution required the knowledge of a lawyer or a judge. The specific task of Gardner's system was to process a typical contract law problem given to first-year law school students:

On July 1 Buyer sent the following telegram to Seller: "Have customers for salt and need carload immediately. Will you supply carload at $2.40 cwt?" Seller received the telegram the same day.

On July 12 Seller sent Buyer the following telegram, which Buyer received the same day: "Accept your offer carload of salt, immediate shipment, terms cash on delivery."

On July 13 Buyer sent by Air Mail its standard form "Purchase Order" to Seller. On the face of the form Buyer had written that it accepted "Seller's offer of July 12" and had written "One carload" and "$2.40 per cwt." in the appropriate spaces for quantity and price. Among numerous printed provisions on the reverse of the form was the following: "Unless otherwise stated on the face hereof, payment on all purchase orders shall not be due until 30 days following delivery." There was no statement on the face of the form regarding time of payment.

Later on July 13 another party offered to sell Buyer a carload of salt for $2.30 per cwt. Buyer immediately wired Seller: "Ignore purchase order mailed earlier today; your offer of July 12 rejected." This telegram was received by Seller on the same day (July 13). Seller received Buyer's purchase order in the mail the following day (July 14).

Briefly analyze each of the items of correspondence in terms of its legal effect, and indicate what the result will be in Seller's action against Buyer for breach of contract. (Gardner, 1987, pp. 4–5)

Knowledge Representation in Gardner's Legal Reasoning Program

The representation of knowledge in legal reasoning programs is difficult because the law and legal analysis involve the complexities, uncertainties, and inconsistencies of everyday human activity. A parallel problem is found in research concerned with the development of computer psychotherapy programs that attempt to model the free-flowing communication of psychotherapy interviews (Wagman, 1980, 1984a, 1984b, 1988; Wagman and Kerber, 1980, 1984).

Even for the relatively simple problem in contract law that the program was to analyze (presented above), Gardner (1987) found it necessary to develop a complex knowledge hierarchy to represent the facts of the case, and a set of 100 rules with which to reason about the facts. Figures 2.4 and 2.5 depict the knowledge hierarchy.

Performance of the Gardner Legal Reasoning Program

The program's analysis of the law school examination problem on contracts (presented above) will be discussed in the present section. The program achieved a total of nine analyses of the examination problem. The summary-level decision tree containing the paths of the

Figure 2.4
Elements of the Abstraction Hierarchy: Part 1.

- Event
    - Simple-event
        - Act
            - Ordinary-act
                - Transfer
                    - Begin-transfer
                        - Send
                            - Mail
                        - Ship
                    - End-transfer
                        - Receive
                        - Deliver
                    - Supply
                - Utter
            - Speech-act
                - Assertion
                - Yes-no-question
                - Request
                - Declaration
            - Legal-act
                - Offer
                    - Counteroffer
                    - Offer-to-modify
                    - Modification-of-offer
                - Acceptance
                - Rejection
                - Revocation
        - Other-simple-event
            - Die
    - Complex-event
        - Exchange
        - Sale

Source: A. Gardner, *An Artificial Intelligence Approach to Legal Reasoning* (Cambridge, MA: MIT Press, 1987), p. 90. Copyright 1987 by the MIT Press. Reprinted with permission.

analyses is depicted in Figure 2.6. In that figure, the analyses that result from the traversal of decision paths appear as the terminal states of the augmented transition network: There is no contract in state 1 or state 0; there is a contract in state 2. Figures 2.7 and 2.8 depict the details of each of the nine analyses of the examination

Figure 2.5
Elements of the Abstraction Hierarchy: Part 2

- State
    - Have
    - Need
    - Want
- Symbolic-object
    - Sentence
    - Proposition
- Physical-thing
    - Physical-object
        - Animate-object
            - Human
        - Inanimate-object
            - Document
                - Telegram
                - Letter
                - Form-document
            - Building
                - House
    - Physical-substance
        - Salt
        - Seed
        - Money
        - Land
- Measure
    - Volume
        - Carloads
        - Barrels
        - Bushels
    - Weight
        - Pounds
        - Cwt
    - Value
        - Dollars
- Time
    - Time-point
    - Time-line
    - Time-interval

Source: A. Gardner, *An Artificial Intelligence Approach to Legal Reasoning* (Cambridge, MA: MIT Press, 1987), p. 91. Copyright 1987 by the MIT Press. Reprinted with permission.

Figure 2.6
Condensed Version of Summary-Level Decision Tree

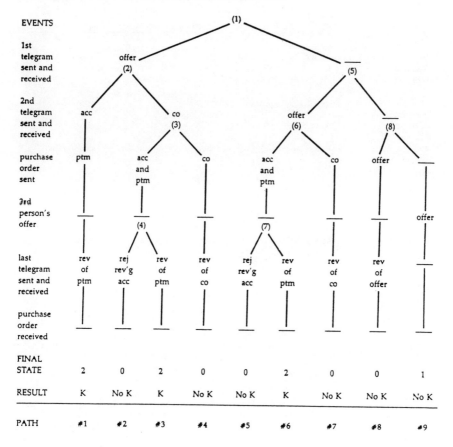

Abbreviations:
  acc - acceptance
  co - counteroffer
  ptm - proposal to modify the contract
  rev - revocation
  rej - rejection
  rej rev'g acc - rejection of offer, revoking a previous acceptance of the offer
  K - contract

Source: A. Gardner: *An Artificial Intelligence Approach to Legal Reasoning* (Cambridge, MA: MIT Press, 1987), p. 176. Copyright 1987 by the MIT Press. Reprinted with permission.

Figure 2.7
Analyses 1 through 4 of the Test Problem

EVENT	PATH #1	#2	#3	#4
1st telegram sent	0 offer 1	0 offer 1	0 offer 1	0 offer 1
1st telegram received				
2nd telegram sent	1 acceptance 2	1 counteroffer 1	1 counteroffer 1	1 counteroffer 1
2nd telegram received				
purchase order sent	2 proposal to modify (ptm) 12	1 acceptance plus ptm 12	1 acceptance plus ptm 12	1 counteroffer 1
3rd person's offer				
last telegram sent	12 provisional revocation of ptm 12	12 provisional rejection of counteroffer, revoking acceptance 12	12 provisional revocation of ptm 12	1 provisional revocation of counteroffer 1
last telegram received	12 revocation confirmed 2	12 rejection confirmed 0	12 revocation confirmed 2	1 revocation confirmed 0
purchase order received				
CONCLUSIONS	State 2: Contract	State 0: No contract	State 2: Contract	State 0: No contract

Source: A. Gardner, *An Artificial Intelligence Approach to Legal Reasoning* (Cambridge, MA: MIT Press, 1987), p. 178. Copyright 1987 by the MIT Press. Reprinted with permission.

problem. They depict the state of the augmented transition network prior to and following the analysis of one of the main events of the examination problem. Events determined by the program to be legally ineffective are represented as blank entries in the state network.

In Figure 2.6, there are eight nodes or choice points that result in nine analyses as described below:

Figure 2.8
Analyses 5 through 9 of the Test Problem

PATH

#5	#6	#7	#8	#9
0 offer 1	0 offer 1	0 offer 1		
1 acceptance plus ptm 12	1 acceptance plus ptm 12	1 counteroffer 1	0 offer 1	
				0 offer 1
12 provisional rejection of offer, revoking acceptance 12	12 provisional revocation of ptm 12	1 provisional revocation of counteroffer 1	1 provisional revocation of offer 1	
12 rejection confirmed 0	12 revocation confirmed 2	1 revocation confirmed 0	1 revocation confirmed 0	
State 0: No contract	State 2: Contract	State 0: No contract	State 0: Contract	State 1: No contract

Source: A. Gardner, *An Artificial Intelligence Approach to Legal Reasoning* (Cambridge, MA: MIT Press, 1987), p. 179. Copyright 1987 by the MIT Press. Reprinted with permission.

1. Is the first telegram an offer, or is it only a preliminary inquiry?

2. Assume the first telegram is an offer. Is the second telegram an acceptance, or is it a counteroffer?

3. Assume the first telegram is an offer and the second a counteroffer. Is the purchase order an acceptance of the counteroffer, with a concomitant proposal to modify the contract, or is the purchase order a further counteroffer?

4. Assume the first telegram is an offer, the second telegram is a counteroffer, and the purchase order is an acceptance (with proposal to modify). Did the final telegram revoke the acceptance and reject the offer?

5. Assume the first telegram is not an offer. Is the second telegram an offer?

6/7. Assume the first telegram is a preliminary inquiry but the second one is an offer. The same questions arise as in 3 and 4.

8. Assume neither of the first two telegrams is an offer. Is the purchase order an offer? (Gardner, 1987, p. 177)

Comparison of the program's legal analyses with that of human lawyers is interesting, as it suggests a fundamental difference in mode of cognition between computer jurisprudence and human jurisprudence:

This list of choices is somewhat larger than a human lawyer would be likely to consider explicitly. [The examination problem] suggested four analyses, not nine. On the other hand, the transition network has an average branching factor of 5.25, so that the space of possible analyses for a nine-event problem is on the order of 5^9, even ignoring such complications as the possibility of finding multiple reasons for taking the same arc.

Of the extra analyses generated by the program, three arise because the program is not yet able to conclude that treating the first telegram as an offer that expired is equivalent in this problem to treating it as a preliminary inquiry. With some additional knowledge, expansion of the tree could be discontinued below node 6 of [Figure 2.6] on the ground of its similarity to node 3. The other two extra analyses reflect the possibility that the second telegram, as well as the first, is only preliminary negotiation. There is a plausible legal foundation for recognizing this possibility. (Gardner, 1987, p. 177, italics added)

The program's reasoning and the effect of its limited legal knowledge (for example, it does not know about the concept of breach of contract) is exemplified in its analysis of events 6, 7, 8, and 9 of the examination problem:

Event 6: Later on July 13 another party offered to sell Buyer a carload of salt for $2.30 per cwt.

Although event 6 stipulates that there is an offer, the program looks for such a stipulation only in state 0. In state 1 the program tries to construe the event as an action on the offer already pending. Correctly, it fails, and the "ineffective event" arc is taken. Still in state 1, the program considers the final telegram.

Event 7: Buyer immediately wired Seller: "Ignore purchase order mailed earlier today; your offer of July 12 rejected."

Event 8: This telegram was received by Seller on the same day (July 13).

Event 9: Seller received Buyer's purchase order in the mail the following day (July 14).

Because the agent of event 7, Buyer is the offeror of the pending offer, the arcs worth trying are quickly reduced to those for revocation or modification of the offer. The revocation rule succeeds, with the declaration of rejection as the needed expression of unwillingness to enter an exchange. Since the telegram gives no description of this exchange, a match with the exchange proposed by the offer is assumed. The consequent of the revocation rule then uses the result from a secondary antecedent: sending a telegram does not count as instantaneous communication; therefore the revocation should not take effect until (and unless) it is received. Accordingly the rule returns a result of provisional success rather than full success. Event 7 is concluded with the transition network still in state 1 but with a transition pending for the revocation. At event 8 the receipt of the telegram confirms the transition, back to state 0. Event 9, receipt of the purchase order, has no effect.

Now consider the other case below node 3 of [Figure 2.6]. Buyer, by sending the purchase order, has accepted an offer and also has proposed a modification of the contract with respect to the time of payment. The transition network is in state 12, with both the existing bargain and the proposed modification represented in the registers. The set of arcs available is somewhat different from those in the previous case. In particular it includes an arc for revocation of an acceptance, rejecting the previous offer instead. This arc has the second example of a competing rule set.

On one branch of the detailed tree, the rule allowing such an act is tried. The rule succeeds after checking, among other things, that Seller has not yet received the purchase order informing him of the acceptance. Since a rejection, like a revocation, is not effective until received, the result is again a pending transition, later confirmed by event 8. As an incidental effect, the proposal to modify the contract is also revoked.

On the other branch, the competing rule says in effect that an acceptance can never be undone. On this branch, the program goes on to consider whether the telegram could be a revocation of the proposal to modify the contract, and the revocation rule succeeds. *If the program knew about breaches of contract, then it would be able to reach a stronger conclusion here: that the final telegram repudiated the existing contract. But the program deals only with contract formation, and revocation of the proposal to modify is therefore the strongest conclusion available about event 7 if withdrawal of one's acceptance is not permitted.* (Gardner, 1987, pp. 180–181, italics added)

The significant effect on the program's reasoning of the lack of a state of representation of ordinary discourse (as distinguished from representation of legal discourse) becomes apparent in the following account of its behavior at choice points 6 and 7 of the decision tree of Figure 2.6:

Choices 6 and 7. At nodes 6 and 7 the choices are similar to those at nodes 3 and 4. *Their presence, however, points up an element that is missing from the current program and that should be supplied in a future version. This element is a representation of the state of the discourse, separate from the representation of the legal state.*

On the paths considered earlier—those on the left-hand side of the tree of [Figure 2.6]—the need for such a distinction was not obvious. On these paths every document has some legal effect. The characterization of each document in terms of its legal effect, along with the findings made in the course of reaching that characterization, preserves most of the relevant information about what the document contributes to the conversation.

On the right-hand side of the tree, on the other hand, the first document exchanged is found not to be an offer. With the network still in state 0, the program considers the second document as if it were the beginning of the conversation. This means that at node 6, where the second telegram is found to be the initial offer, the terms of this offer are computed without cumulating them with what went before. Thus its terms are not identical with those of the counteroffer found at node 3. For this reason, terminating expansion of the tree at node 6 would require a significant conceptual addition to the program. (Gardner, 1987, pp. 181–182, italics added)

Commentary on Computer Jurisprudence

It is important to recognize a fundamental distinction between expert systems in science and technology (Buchanan, 1982; Feigenbaum, 1977a) and expert systems in jurisprudence. The former represent or strive for consensual validation; the latter must cope with competing rules and the expectation of varying interpretation, argumentation, and judicial decision. Gardner's (1987) legal reasoning program wisely attempted the separation of clear legal issues which the program could decide by deductive reasoning and hard legal issues which require for their argumentation, elucidation, and resolution, the beliefs, purposes, knowledge, and cognitive and affective processes of human lawyers and human judges. The methods of artificial intelligence used by Gardner successfully modelled first-year law school students in identifying issues in a well-defined examination problem in contract law, but it remains to be seen whether new methods in artificial intelligence (Grimson and Patil, 1987; Wagman, in press) can successfully model the human intelligence that enters into legal interpretation and disputation and that culminates in a correct judicial decision.

RATIONALITY AND HUMAN COGNITION

The Concept of Rationality

The major problem in the study of human rationality has been the tension between rationality construed as an abstract, ideal, and formal systematization, and rationality construed as concrete, real, contextually embedded, and ideographic. The former has been taken as the normative standard against which to judge the latter. The normative standard of syllogistic logic was developed by Aristotle (384–322 B.C.) to evaluate the rationality of philosophical and political argumentation. The normative standard of mathematical proof was developed by Euclid (300 B.C.) to evaluate the rationality of geometric and arithmetic reasoning. The mathematical equations of Galileo Galilei (1564–1642), Johannes Kepler (1571–1630), and Sir Isaac Newton (1642–1727) were normative standards against which to evaluate the rationality of conceptions about the physical universe.

The philosophical enlightenment, as heir to Newton's rational universe, sought in the formulations of David Hume (1711–1776), Adam Smith (1723–1790), and George Boole (1815–1864) to establish the rational nature of the human mind (Sampson, 1956). Rationality as an ideal, perfect, and eternal state was posited by Plato (Merlan, 1960) and ascribed by Bertrand Russell (1872–1970) to his system of symbolic logic (Russell and Whitehead, 1910), but Russell (1948, 1967) was careful to distinguish his abstract system from being, in any way, descriptive of his own or anyone else's ordinary, nontechnical, everyday reasoning. Russell held that symbolic logic would exist even if there were no human minds.

Modern experimental psychology has regularly studied human rationality and has used the normative standards of logic and mathematics to evaluate everyday reasoning. This research and its conclusion regarding the rationality of the human mind will be discussed in the present section, following an examination of the abstract concepts of the rational human as used in classical and neoclassical theory in economic science, and of mathematical theory as the example, par excellence, of abstract and ideal rationality.

Rationality and Economics

Classical and neoclassical economics provides an excellent example of the tension, discussed above, between human rationality as predicated in abstract systems and as observed in real institutional and individual behavior. The formulations of classical economics (Smith, [1776] 1985) postulate perfect competition and rational, logical, and self-regulating mechanisms that govern markets and insure equilibrating prices; and the formulations of neoclassical economics (Friedman, 1962) couch these postulates as complex and abstruse sets of descriptive and deductive mathematical equations.

However, classical and neoclassical economic theory, even when wrapped in the cloak of mathematics, falls abysmally short (Leontief, 1982) of the descriptive and predictive power displayed by classical and neoclassical theories of the physical universe. The rationality of Newtonian mechanics and its descriptions via simple mathematical equations was appropriate to the relatively simple and universal conditions of physical force, acceleration, mass, distance, and gravitation; but its limitation in classical and neoclassical economics was and is inappropriate to the mixed, inconsistent, and fluctuating conditions of institutional markets, financial currencies, taxation policies, government involvement, labor union activity, cultural trends, and complex motivations of individual consumers in patterns of saving and consumption (Leontief, 1982).

That empirically determined economic conditions of the marketplace and of individual psychology do not support the formal mathematical models has had little or no effect on the doctrines of neoclassical economics that dominate research journals in economics (Leontief, 1982). It would appear that the doctrine of the rational economic human is rigorously defended because rationality can be modelled by formal deductive and mathematical schemes (Freudenthal, 1961) and that production of these abstractions becomes an end in itself. Rationality and mathematical formalization are also found in the physical sciences, but scientific epistemology provides for the experimental testing of theory, the falsifiability of doctrine by empirical observation, the revision of the formal theory and its mathematical representation in response to the data, and the continuing cycle of investigation that intends not a protection of doctrine but a more exact and complete account of nature.

W. Leontief (1982), a major contributor to the development of contemporary economics, provided the following interesting comments on the tension between economics as formal rational science, replete with abstract mathematical models, and economics as the applied, concrete study of the actual variables that characterize the real economic system:

Two hundred years ago the founders of modern economic science — Adam Smith, Ricardo, Malthus, and John Stuart Mill — erected an imposing conceptual edifice based on the notion of the national economy as a self-regulating system of a great many different but interrelated, and therefore, interdependent, activities; a concept so powerful and fruitful that it gave impetus to Charles Darwin's pathbreaking work on his theory of evolution.

The central idea of what is now being referred to as Classical Economics attracted the attention of two mathematically trained engineers, Leon Walras and Vilfredo Pareto, who translated it with considerable refinement and elaboration into a concise language of algebra and calculus and called it the General Equilibrium Theory. Under the name of neoclassical economics this theory now constitutes the core of undergraduate and graduate instruction in this country.

As an empirical science, economics dealt from the outset with phenomena of common experience. Producing and consuming goods, buying and selling, and receiving income and spending it are activities engaging everyone's attention practically all the time. Even the application of the scientific principle of quantification did not have to be initiated by the analyst himself — measuring and pricing constitute an integral part of the phenomena that he sets out to explain. Herein lies, however, the initial source of the trouble in which academic economics finds itself today.

By the time the facts of everyday experience were used up, economists were able to turn for bits and pieces of less accessible, more specialized information to government statistics. However, these statistics — compiled for administrative or business, but not scientific, purposes — fall short of what would have been required for concrete, more detailed understanding of the structure and the functioning of a modern economic system.

Not having been subjected from the outset to the harsh discipline of systematic fact-finding, traditionally imposed on and accepted by their colleagues in the natural and historical sciences, economists developed a nearly irresistible predilection for deductive reasoning. As a matter of fact, many entered the field after specializing in pure or applied mathematics. Page after page of professional economic journals are filled with mathematical formulas leading the reader from sets of more or less plausible but entirely arbitrary assumptions to precisely stated but irrelevant theoretical conclusions.

Nothing reveals the aversion of the great majority of the present-day academic economists for systematic empirical inquiry more than the methodological devices that they employ to avoid or cut short the use of concrete factual information. Instead of constructing theoretical models capable of preserving the identity of hundreds, even thousands, of variables needed for the concrete description and analysis of a modern economy, they first of all resort to "aggregation." The primary information, however detailed, is packaged in a relatively small number of bundles labeled "Capital," "Labor," "Raw Materials," "Intermediate Goods," "General Price Level," and so on. These bundles are then usually fitted into a "model," that is, a small system of equations describing the entire economy in terms of a small number of corresponding "aggregative" variables. The fitting, as a rule, is accomplished by means of "least squares" or another similar curve-fitting procedure. . . .

Hence, while the labels attached to symbolic variables and parameters of the theoretical equations tend to suggest that they could be identified with those directly observable in the real world, any attempt to do so is bound to fail: the problem of "identification" of aggregative equations after they have been reduced — that is, transformed, as they often are — for purposes of the curve-fitting process, was raised many years ago but still has not found a satisfactory solution. In the meantime, the procedure described above was standardized to such an extent that, to carry out a respectable econometric study, one simply had to construct a plausible and easily computable theoretical model and then secure — mostly from secondary or tertiary sources — a set of time series or cross section data related in some direct or indirect way to its particular subject, insert these figures with a program of an appropriate statistical routine taken from the shelf into the computer, and finally publish the computer printouts with a more or less plausible interpretation of the numbers. . . .

Year after year economic theorists continue to produce scores of mathematical models and to explore in great detail their formal properties; and the econometricians fit algebraic functions of all possible shapes to essentially the same sets of data without being able to advance, in any perceptible way, a systematic understanding of the structure and the operations of a real economic system. (adapted from Leontief, 1982, pp. 104, 107)

The Rationality of Mathematical Abstraction and Mathematical Idealization

In order to solve problems regarding physical objects, simplifying assumptions about the physical object are made, the essential characteristics are mathematically abstracted, and the problem is then represented as a mathematical idealization in the form of, for example, sets of differential equations; finally, the solution to these equations is projected back into the physical world where it constitutes the solution to the original problem. If the simplifying assumptions required for mathematical abstraction and mathematical idealization are too drastic, the mathematical solution will be only approximate and, perhaps, may be completely unsatisfactory. Simplifying the contextual complexities of a physical problem may permit mathematical abstraction, idealization, and solution, but this entire mathematical modelling process (Iliev, 1972) will not insure a precise and complete solution in the world of real objects if the contextual complexity of the problem has been distorted and oversimplified.

There is, thus, a tension between the rationality of abstract systematization and the contextual complexities of the real world, as was discussed above, and as will be discussed below in the section on research in the psychology of rationality, where the issue of the quality of human rationality is examined. To anticipate that examination, the thesis will be advanced that the criterion of formal rationality in judging reasoning about real-world psychological problems that are contextually embedded becomes increasingly weak, misleading, and unsatisfactory, as oversimplifying assumptions are increasingly introduced that permit the rational analysis at the cost of distorting the contextual complexities of the psychological problem.

In order to assist in the understanding of this thesis regarding abstract rationality and psychological reasoning (where intangible moods, fleeting feelings, and mixed attitudes interact with planning, judging, remembering, and thinking), it will be useful to consider the structurally analogous thesis discussed in this section concerning the relationship between the process of mathematical abstraction and idealization and the simplification of assumptions regarding complex conditions of physical problems, as described by S. L. Ross (1964):

Assumptions in Mathematical Abstraction and Idealization

We now make certain assumptions concerning the string, its vibrations, and its surroundings. To begin with, we assume that the string is perfectly flexible, is of constant linear density ρ, and is of constant tension T at all times. Concerning the vibrations, we assume that the motion is confined to the xy plane and that each point on the string moves on a straight line perpendicular to the x axis as the string vibrates. Further, we assume that the displacement y at each point of the string is small compared to the length L and that the angle between the string and the x axis at each point is also sufficiently small. Finally, we assume that no external forces (such as damping forces, for example) act upon the string.

Although these assumptions are not actually valid in any physical problem, nevertheless they are approximately satisfied in many cases. They are

made in order to make the resulting mathematical problem more tractable.
With these assumptions, then, the problem is to find the displacement y as a
function of x and t.

Under the assumptions stated it can be shown that the displacement y
satisfies the *partial differential equation,*

$$\alpha^2 \frac{\delta^2 y}{\delta x^2} = \frac{\delta^2 y}{\delta t^2} \; ,$$

where $\alpha^2 = T/\rho$. This is the one-dimensional wave equation. (Ross, 1964, pp.
525–526, italics added)

Deductive Structure and Descriptive Reality

For two millennia, Euclidean geometry was considered both a deductive structure, consisting of axioms and logically derived theorems, and a description of real-world geometric relationships. These
dual aspects of the Euclidean system made its axiomatic structure
and its applications appear to be self-evident, unviolable, and inevi-
table (Bowne, 1966). The development of non-Euclidean geometries
in the nineteenth century was greeted with disbelief and deep misgiv-
ings, as it seemed to threaten the intellectual structure of mathematics and science (Greenberg, 1974). In its aftermath, non-Euclidean
geometry resulted in the recasting of the nature of mathematics.
Mathematics was seen as a formal intellectual discipline in which different systems of axioms could be constructed that would result in the
proof of different theorems and in different descriptions of real-
world geometry (Golos, 1968).

In Euclidean geometry, the statement that "Given a line in a plane
and a point in the plane not on the line, only one line can be drawn
through the given point parallel to the given line," appeared to be
both axiomatically self-evident and descriptive of real-world geometry. In Lobachevskian geometry, one of two major non-Euclidean geometries, an axiom is proposed that contradicts the sacrosanct
Euclidean parallel postulate and contravenes experience and mea-
surement in real-world geometry: "At least two lines can be drawn
through a given point parallel to a given line." In Riemannian geometry, the other major non-Euclidean geometry, an axiom is proposed
that results in sets of theorems and mensuration properties that differ, in various respects, from both Lobachevskian geometry and Euclidean geometry: "No line can be drawn through a given point
parallel to a given line." Table 2.1 intercompares the Euclidean, Lobachevskian, and Riemannian systems of geometry.

Table 2.1
Comparison of Euclidean and Non-Euclidean Geometries

	Euclidean	Lobachevskian	Riemannian	
Two distinct lines intersect in	at most one	at most one	one (single elliptic) two (double elliptic)	point points
Given line L and point P not on L, there exist	one and only one line	at least two lines	no lines	through P parallel to L
A line	is	is	is not	separated into two parts by a point
Parallel lines	are equidistant	are never equidistant	do not exist	
If a line intersects one of two parallel lines, it	must	may or may not	—	intersect the other
The valid Saccheri hypothesis is the	right angle	acute angle	obtuse angle	hypothesis
Two distinct lines perpendicular to the same line	are parallel	are parallel	intersect	
The angle sum of a triangle is	equal to	less than	greater than	180 degrees
The area of a triangle is	independent	proportional to the defect	proportional to the excess	of its angle sum
Two triangles with equal corresponding angles are	similar	congruent	congruent	

Source: W. Prenowitz and M. Jordan, *Basic Concepts of Geometry* (New York: Cambridge University Press), p. 222.

In Table 2.1, axiomatic differences in the three systems are indicated in the second line. Deductions from the different axioms lead to different properties of triangles as indicated in the final three lines of the table. Different geometric deductive structures lead to different descriptions of real-world geometry.

Deductive structures and descriptive reality may co-vary, as just discussed, but they may also be independent. Formal mathematics is the logical deduction and proof of theorems (Curry, 1951). Technically, formal mathematics is a logical structure; it has no meaning within itself and often has no application as a description of the real world.

In economics, as in mathematics, formal deductive structures may or may not have applications as descriptions of economic behavior (see the section on rationality and economics). Where economic models are not autonomously formal, the situation resembles Euclidean geometry, in that neoclassical economics is held to be both a deductive structure and a description of real-world economic behavior. As in the case of the comparison among Euclidean and non-Euclidean geometries, presented above, different deductive economic structures may lead to different descriptions of economic reality, so that just as the properties of triangles may be familiar or strange, so the properties of institutions and markets may be familiar or strange. The analysis of geometric and economic deductive structures and their application or nonapplication as descriptions of reality is extended in a later section to research and theory in the psychology of rationality and reasoning.

Rationality and the Concept of the Infinitesimal

The concept of the infinitesimal offers another perspective on the tension between rationality as abstract, ideal, and formal, and rationality as empirical and utilitarian. The classical Greek philosophers rejected the concept of the infinitesimal, along with the concept of the infinite, as lacking in logic and deviating from ordinary reality and experience (Guggenheimer, 1977). The concept was abstract, ideal, and self-contradictory: a number infinitely small, but nevertheless, greater than zero. Both Newton (1642–1727) and Leibniz (1646–1716) recognized the logical difficulties inherent in the concept of the infinitesimal; nevertheless, they proceeded to develop the infinitesimal calculus, which has had widespread application in science and engineering. However, mathematicians of the nineteenth century were interested in establishing sound logical foundations for the calculus and, following Karl Weierstrass (1815–1897), they excluded the infinitesimal from a reconstrued calculus that became standard analysis (Dieudonne, 1971). In the twentieth century, A. Robinson (1966) developed nonstandard analysis, a system of mathematical logic that includes infinitesimals.

The infinitesimal calculus of Newton and Leibniz derives from the problem of understanding the motion of a falling object and determining the relationships between the instantaneous position of the object and its instantaneous velocity, using the concepts of infinitesimal increments of time (dt) and infinitesimal increments of distance (*ds*). The finite instantaneous velocity of the falling object is the ratio *ds/dt*, and *ds/dt* = 32 + 16*dt*.

The paradox arises that the equation is composed on the left-hand side of a finite quantity and on the right-hand side of a finite quantity plus an infinitesimal quantity. We would, therefore, arbitrarily have to drop 16*dt* in order to obtain the desired finite instantaneous velocity of 32 feet per second. Indeed, both Newton and Leibniz did drop 16*dt*, by setting *dt* = 0. This mathematical operation was followed by subsequent mathematicians into the nineteenth century, although the logical objections of Bishop George Berkeley (1685–1753) were recognized. Berkeley objected:

"It should seem that this reasoning is not fair or conclusive." After all, dt is either equal to zero or not equal to zero. If dt is not zero, then 32 + 16dt is not the same as 32. If dt is zero, then the increment in distance ds is also zero, and the fraction ds/dt is not 32 + 16dt but a meaningless expression, 0/0. For when it is said, let the increments vanish, i.e., let the increments be nothing, or let there be no increments, the former supposition that the increments were something, or that there were increments, is destroyed, and yet a consequence of that supposition, i.e., an expression got by virtue thereof, is retained. Which is a false way of reasoning. (Berkeley, [1734] 1929, p. 244)

The logical complications of the infinitesimal calculus did not interfere with applied mathematics, but pure mathematics could not countenance the infinitesimal and, in a way, Euclid and Aristotle were vindicated. The mathematicians of the nineteenth century replaced the concept of infinitesimals with the concept of limits.

In the method of limits, the instantaneous velocity of a falling object is defined as a limit that can be approximated by ratios of finite increments (not infinitesimals). The ratio of the variable finite distance increment Δs to the variable finite time increment Δt is the variable finite velocity, 32 + 16Δt. As Δt takes on smaller and smaller values, the ratio $\Delta s/\Delta t$ approaches the limit of 32 feet per second, at $t = 1$ second. Note that, in the method of limits, the procedure of setting $\Delta t = 0$ is not directly used.

In the twentieth century, advances in symbolic logic by Bertrand Russell and A. N. Whitehead (1910) and by Abraham Robinson (1964, 1969) led to an increased formalization of mathematics and, in the system of nonstandard analysis developed by Robinson (1966), to the reinstatement of infinitesimals. Robinson's achievement depended on the use of the theory of formal languages. In contrast to natural languages, formal languages possess strict vocabularies and rules that limit what is expressible in the language (as in the case of computer languages). Robinson (1966) reviewed Leibniz's work on the use of the infinitesimals ds/dt in solving the problem of instantaneous velocity and Leibniz's recognition of the philosophical problem of the use of the infinitesimal calculus, as well as the criticisms advanced by Berkeley and discussed above. Robinson demonstrated how his method of nonstandard analysis provided for reinterpretations of the infinitesimal in a context of symbolic logic that results in a precise resolution of the historic controversies about infinitesimals.

Leibniz claimed that the soundness of his system of infinitesimal calculus did not depend on the demonstrable existence of infinitesimals, but only on their assumed ("as if") existence. The system was sound in that it produced correct solutions to physical problems, but the concept of the infinitesimal was anything but clear. Infinitesimal numbers and real numbers were given equivalent properties, the property of being positive or negative, for instance. Thus, infinitesimals belonged to the class of positive numbers, but yet were infinitely smaller than any real positive number.

The contradictory nature of infinitesimals was resolved by Robinson's (1966) use of a formal language in which properties of infinitesimals and properties of real numbers can be expressed, but in which certain properties cannot be expressed, such as the property of being both positive and smaller than any real positive number.

In Robinson's system of nonstandard analysis, there are two conceptual universes of mathematical objects. The standard universe contains the system of ordinary real numbers, the calculus, and the topics of mathematical analysis. The nonstandard universe contains all that is in the standard universe plus infinitesimals and infinite numbers.

Robinson applied nonstandard analysis to the problem of computing the instantaneous velocity of a falling object. The terms ds, and dt, and their ratio, ds/dt, are used in the computation, but they are interpreted differently. The standard part of the ratio ds/dt is defined as the instantaneous velocity. The terms ds/dt and dt are interpreted as nonstandard real numbers.

In the equation $ds/dt = 32 + 16dt$, the velocity, which is the standard part of ds/dt and the value we are seeking, equals 32, because $16dt$ is a nonstandard number. In other words, we are matching or equating a standard number (32) on the right-hand side of the equation with a standard number (the instantaneous velocity) on the left-hand side. As Robinson (1966) indicated, clear delineation between standard and nonstandard numbers, the standard and nonstandard parts of *ds/dt,* avoids the confusion of Leibniz's infinitesimals.

Where Leibniz, Bishop Berkeley, and others worried about the real existence of infinitesimals, the use of formal languages permits an interpretation of existence simply to mean it is expressible or unexpressible in the sentences of the language. A symbolic logic has finessed the philosophical disputations concerning the existence of infinitesimals. Infinitesimals are precisely defined in a formal language structure, and Robinson (1966) has demonstrated that their use results in a more lucid and more powerful proof of theorems in many areas of contemporary formal mathematics.

It is interesting that despite the sophistications of mathematical logic, formal languages, and nonstandard analysis, which permit advances in rational power far beyond the achievements of previous centuries, there is a sense in which the concept of the infinitesimal and the infinite (Bolzano, 1950; Hilbert, 1964; Stroyan and Luxemberg, 1976; Zippin, 1962) remains a mystery beyond human rationality. Compare, for example, the following quotations by the Renaissance mathematician Nicholas of Cusa (1450), the mathematician Blaise Pascal (1623–1662), and the astronomer-mathematician Johannes Kepler (1571–1630), with the limitations of human rationality as expressed by the mathematical logician, Abraham Robinson (1918–1974):

[The infinite is] the source and means, and at the same time the unattainable goal, of all knowledge. (Nicholas of Cusa, quoted in David and Hersh, 1981, p. 241)

Nature teaches geometry by instinct alone, even without ratiocination [about infinitesimals]. (Johannes Kepler, quoted in Davis and Hersh, 1981, p. 241)

In answering those of his contemporaries who objected to reasoning with infinitely small quantities, Pascal was fond of saying that the heart intervenes to make the work clear. Pascal looked on the infinitely large and the infinitely small as mysteries, something that nature has proposed to man not for him to understand but for him to admire. (Davis and Hersh, 1981, p. 241)

I cannot imagine that I shall ever return to the creed of the true Platonist, who sees the world of the actual infinite spread out before him and believes that he can comprehend the incomprehensible. (Robinson, quoted in Davis and Hersh, 1981, p. 319)

Rationality and Psychological Research

In previous sections, rationality has been examined in various contexts and with respect to tensions and antinomies between rationality as formal deductive structure and rationality as descriptive reality. In the present section, the tensions concerning the two versions of rationality are examined in the context of psychological research. In particular, the research of D. Kahneman and A. Tversky (Kahneman, Slovic, and Tversky, 1982; Kahneman and Tversky, 1982, 1984; Tversky and Kahneman, 1983) will be discussed in a series of examples drawn from that research, with emphasis on the nature of the assumptions, interpretations, abstractions, criteria, and conclusions regarding human rationality.

Example One

Two groups of subjects were told either (group A) that on the way to the theatre they have lost tickets that cost 40 dollars, or (group B) that on the way to the theatre they have lost cash in the amount of 40 dollars. The groups were asked if they would buy new tickets. Group A responded that they would less frequently than group B. Spending 80 dollars in a "theatre-going" account was too extravagant. Group B subjects assigned their loss to a "general cash" account, which was not tied specifically to theatre tickets.

The researchers asserted that group A and group B should not respond differently because the totality of expenditures (80 dollars) would be identical. Clearly, this is an example of inappropriate mathematical abstraction which dissolved the differentiated cognitive structures (theatre-going account and general cash account) of subjects (see section 2 of Table 2.2) and an inappropriate imposition of a criterion of abstract rationality (see section 5 of Table 2.2).

Example Two

Subjects were given a description of a 31-year-old woman, and then were asked to assign probability estimates to statements concerning her. The description included the information that as a college student, she had majored in philosophy, was intensely interested in issues concerned with social equity, and had actively participated in antinuclear and antidiscrimination demonstrations. Subjects were asked to rank a set of eight statements from "most probable" to "least probable." Included in the set were the items: (a) She is a bank teller and active in the feminist movement, (b) she is a bank teller, and (c) she is a psychiatric social worker.

Table 2.2
Problematic Assumptions, Abstractions, and Conclusions in the Kahneman and Tversky Research on the Psychology of Rationality

I. *FOCUS OF STUDY*

The focus of study should be defining, describing, and measuring actual human reasoning with psychological problem, rather than mathematical abstraction and idealization of the psychological problem.

II. *MATHEMATICAL ABSTRACTION*

The mathematical abstraction of the psychological problem requires drastic assumptions that essentially eliminate the psychological conditions of the human reasoner, which were supposed to be the object of the study.

III. *SELECTION OF MATHEMATICAL STRUCTURES*

The particular mathematical formulae used by Kahneman and Tversky represent an arbitrary selection from a broad range of possible formulae. There are many versions of Bayes's theorem and Bayes's equations, and there are many versions of standard and nonstandard mathematical theorems of probability and probability equations (Mackie, 1973).

IV. *APPLICATION OF ACTUARIAL PREDICTION*

The theory of actuarial prediction is based on population samples with application to target sample, with probability statements having referent to the sample, with increasing error as size of the sample diminishes, and with maximum error in application to the single case. Moreover, as the amount of definitive information regarding the single case increases, the value of and need of actuarial prediction diminishes rapidly.

V. *CRITERIA OF RATIONALITY AND ASSOCIATED CONCLUSIONS*

The criterion of adherence to abstract deductive structures is inappropriate and results in the unwarranted conclusion that human rationality is, in general, of low quality. The transformation of a complex psychological problem constituted of affective, conative, cognitive, situational, and cultural interacting components into a rationalized mathematical problem whose solution becomes the criterion for solution of the psychological problem and from which conclusions about human reasoning with psychological problems are drawn is, altogether, a highly dubious process.

The researchers found that 80 percent of the subjects ranked the first item as more probable than the second item, and concluded that this was a violation of rationality because mathematical probability theory stipulates that, given events X and Y, the probability of both X and Y is less than the probability of X alone or the probability of Y alone. According to the researchers, the subjects were biased or in error because they integrated the details of the woman's activist background with the detail of being a feminist. However, this integration of information is not in error, and neither is it in violation of statistical probability, because the information is reasonably linked rather than absolutely independent as required in mathematical abstraction (see section 2 of Table 2.2) and because increased knowledge of the single case renders abstract actuarial prediction less applicable (see section 4 of Table 2.2).

Example Three

Subjects were informed that, in a court case, a witness to a cab crash has identified the cab as green; that under the particular environmental conditions such witnesses can correctly distinguish green cabs from blue cabs 80 percent of the time; and that, in the particular city, the ratio of green cabs to blue cabs is 15 percent/85 percent. The researchers then asked subjects to state the probability that the cab in the crash was actually a blue cab.

For the group of subjects, a median probability of .20 was found. The researchers claimed that the median probability estimate was incorrect because the subjects should have construed the problem as a mathematical abstraction and should have applied a statistical measure that takes account of base rates. In particular, the researchers contended that the subjects should have construed the problem in terms of Bayes's theorem (see Table 2.3), which does take into account base rates or a priori probabilities. In this case, the base rates of green cabs and blue cabs were quite different (15 percent green cabs, 85 percent blue cabs, based on the information given to the subjects).

The researchers (Tversky and Kahneman, 1977) applied Bayes's theorem (Table 2.3), assuming that the a priori probabilities were to be taken into account simply on the basis of the frequency of blue and green cabs and regardless of whether blue and green cabs had any differential accident rates. Thus, the researchers computed the values for the terms in Bayes's equation (5) in Table 2.3 as follows:

$$P(H/E) = \frac{(.2)(.85)}{(.2)(.85) + (.8)(.15)} = \frac{.17}{.29} = .59$$

However, because no information was given regarding differential accident rates for blue and green cabs, their relative frequency can be disregarded, or, following LaPlace's rule, each a priori probability

Table 2.3
A Derivation of Bayes's Theorem

The posterior probability of a hypothesis if given evidence E is

$$P(H|E) = \frac{P(H \cap E)}{P(E)} \tag{1}$$

where $P(H \cap E)$ is the probability of both H and E being true and $P(E)$ is the probability of the evidence. We can express these as

$$P(H \cap E) = P(E|H)P(H) \tag{2}$$

and

$$P(E) = P(H \cap E) + P(\bar{H} \cap E) \tag{3}$$

where

$$P(\bar{H} \cap E) = P(E|\bar{H})P(\bar{H}). \tag{4}$$

In these equations, $P(\bar{H} \cap E)$ denotes the probability of both the hypothesis being false and the evidence still obtaining; $P(E|H)$ is the conditional probability of the evidence if the hypothesis is true; $P(E|\bar{H})$ is the conditional probability of the evidence if the hypothesis is false; $P(H)$ is the prior probability of the hypothesis; and $P(\bar{H}) = 1 - P(H)$. Substituting equations 2, 3 and 4 into equation 1 . . .

$$P(H|E) = \frac{P(E|H)P(H)}{P(E|H)P(H) + P(E|\bar{H})P(\bar{H})} \tag{5}$$

Source: Adapted from J. R. Anderson, *Cognitive Psychology and Its Implications* (2nd ed., New York: W. H. Freeman and Company, 1985), p. 300.

can be assigned a value of .5, in which case, $P(H) = P(\bar{H}) = .5$, and, therefore, the a priori probabilities are cancelled out, yielding:

$$P(H \mid E) = \frac{(.2)(.5)}{(.2)(.5) + (.8)(.5)} = \frac{.2}{.2 + .8} = .2,$$

the median a posteriori probability solution given by subjects.

We have presented the analysis of both the researchers and the subjects in terms of Bayes's theorem. Clearly, the researchers used Bayes's theorem (and used it incorrectly), but it is not at all clear that the subjects used Bayes's theorem, unless it so happened that they were simultaneously taking a course in statistics in which they had recently studied Bayes's equation. Therefore, it is most likely the case that the subjects simply: (a) disregarded the disparity in number of blue and green cabs, feeling it had no bearing; and (b) simply subtracted the correct identification value of .8 from 1.0 to yield the estimate of .2 that the cab was actually blue.

It is important to note that the experiment throws no light on the subjects' actual cognitive processes. It merely shows that they did not follow the experimenters' interpretation and application of Bayes's theorem, and they probably did not use Bayes's theorem at all; but if we want to understand the nature of reasoning in everyday situations or in the way jurors evaluate witnesses' evidence in testimony in a court case, then the focus of research should not be on whether subjects can apply a normative statistical measure (Bayes's equation), but rather on what cognitive processes lead them to or prevent them from taking account of base rates, and how to combine that information with the evaluation of the witnesses' testimony or evidence (see section 1 of Table 2.2).

It is interesting that Tversky and Kahneman (1983), in reviewing their own extensive research involving "more than 3,000 subjects and dozens of problems" (p. 309), reached a conclusion that is in line with the present analysis (see Table 2.2), and asserted that mathematical abstraction, except for "the domain of random sampling" (p. 310) is not an appropriate standard or descriptor of everyday human rationality:

Judgments of probability vary in the degree to which they follow a decompositional or a holistic approach and in the degree to which the assessment and the aggregation of probabilities are analytic or intuitive. . . . At one extreme there are questions (e.g., What are the chances of beating a given hand in poker?) that can be answered by calculating the relative frequency of "favorable" outcomes. Such an analysis possesses all the features associated with an extensional approach: It is decompositional, frequentistic, and algorithmic. At the other extreme, there are questions (e.g., What is the probability that the witness is telling the truth?) that are normally evaluated in a holistic, singular, and intuitive manner. . . . Decomposition and calculation provide some protection against conjunction errors and other biases, *but the intuitive element cannot be entirely eliminated from probability judgments outside the domain of random sampling.* (Tversky and Kahneman, 1983, p. 310, italics added)

The tension between the normative and descriptive accounts of rationality (introduced at the beginning of this section) and the inappropriateness of mathematical or logical modelling of everyday reasoning, discussed in this section (and summarized in Table 2.2) are recognized, reluctantly, by Tversky and Kahneman (1983) in their admission of the problems entailed by a research model that studies deviations from normative mathematical and logical models of reasoning. These are problems that could be obviated by research that studies the actual details of everyday reasoning with its myriad inconsistent, but useful, distinctions of judgments according to idiosyncratic contexts that cannot be modelled by formal mathematical abstractions (see section 1 of Table 2.2):

Our studies of inductive reasoning have focused on systematic errors because they are diagnostic of the heuristics that generally govern judgment and inference. . . . The focus on bias and illusion is a research strategy that exploits human error, although it neither assumes nor entails that people are perceptually or cognitively inept. . . .

We have argued that intuitive judgments of all relevant marginal, conjunctive, and conditional probabilities are not likely to be coherent, that is, to satisfy the constraints of probability theory. . . .

The violations of the qualitative laws of geometry and probability in judgments of distance and likelihood have significant implications for the interpretation and use of these judgments. Incoherence sharply restricts the inferences that can be drawn from subjective estimates. . . . Furthermore, a system of judgments that does not obey the conjunction rule cannot be expected to obey more complicated principles that presuppose this rule, such as Bayesian updating, external calibration, and the maximization of expected utility. *The presence of bias and incoherence does not diminish the normative force of these principles, but it reduces their usefulness as descriptions of behavior and hinders their prescriptive applications. Indeed, the elicitation of unbiased judgments and the reconciliation of incoherent assessments pose serious problems that presently have no satisfactory solution* (Lindley, Tversky & Brown, 1979; Shafer & Tversky, 1981).

The issue of coherence has loomed larger in the study of preference and belief than in the study of perception. . . . In the absence of an objective criterion of validity, the normative theory of judgment under uncertainty has treated the coherence of belief as the touchstone of human rationality. Coherence has also been assumed in many descriptive analyses in psychology, economics, and other social sciences. This assumption is attractive because the strong normative appeal of the laws of probability makes violations appear implausible. Our studies of the conjunction rule show that normatively inspired theories that assume coherence are descriptively inadequate, whereas psychological analyses that ignore the appeal of normative rules are, at best, incomplete. A comprehensive account of human judgment must reflect the tension between compelling logical rules and seductive nonextensional intuitions. (Tversky and Kahneman, 1983, pp. 313–314, italics added)

Conclusion

Formal constructs of rationality vary with respect to their existence as self-contained systems, and with respect to impingement on and interaction with the empirical concerns of science and everyday reasoning. Systems of formal mathematics and formal logic may be essentially autonomous deductive structures with little or no interpretive applications. Systems of mathematics may have intimate and mutually dependent relationships with theoretical and applied science. Mathematical models may be viewed as conceptual tools directed toward the improvement of understanding in physics, economics, and psychology. As discussed above, mathematical modelling of psychological reasoning is especially difficult, and the balancing of formal criteria and heuristic criteria in judging the quality of human rationality constitutes, in itself, a significant and formidable problem in rational analysis.

As self-involved reasoners investigating our own rationality, we may be forever limited by self-recursive cognition and the absence of a comparative standard. However, comparison with the rationality of artificial intelligence may, to some extent and from certain perspectives, obviate the limitation.

THREE

Problem Solving and Knowledge

In the first section of this chapter, the general logic of artificial intelligence approaches to problem solving in the natural sciences is discussed. Problem-solving systems are analyzed at three levels of sophistication. The FERMI system can solve a range of problems in the physical sciences. FERMI's capacity for multi-domain application is a consequence of its hierarchical organization of general principles, specific knowledge, and strategies of problem solving. FERMI's solution of physics problems in the areas of fluid pressure, electric potential, and center of mass is described. The chapter concludes with the problem of whether the logic of artificial intelligence problem-solving systems such as FERMI exerts an ineluctable rigidity that prevents the achievement of a fourth level of development characterized by adaptive ingenuity in problem-solving representations and strategies.

In the second section of the chapter, an account is presented of how artificial intelligence methods are used to analyze the nature of medical problem solving and reasoning in the establishment of cardiological diagnoses. Expert cardiologists were presented with a complex case of bacterial endocarditis. The cardiologists' pathophysiological explanation of the case was analyzed as sets of production rules. The hierarchy of production rules was found to distinguish accurate from inaccurate diagnoses. The section concludes with the problem of whether the production rule methodology can be extended to the discernment of differential reasoning patterns associated with the establishment of effective diagnoses in other areas of medicine.

ARTIFICIAL INTELLIGENCE AND PROBLEM SOLVING IN THE NATURAL SCIENCES

The General Logic of Problem-Solving Systems

The general logic of problem-solving systems has developed, over the course of several decades, at three levels of sophistication. At the first level, exemplified by General Problem Solver (Newell, Shaw, and Simon, 1960), strategic problem-solving methods (e.g., means–ends analysis) were deemed sufficient. However, it soon became apparent that domain-specific knowledge was necessary to solve problems in the natural sciences. At the second level of development, there was a conjunction of problem-solving methods and domain-specific knowledge, as exemplified in chemistry by DENDRAL (Feigenbaum, Buchanan, and Lederberg, 1987) and in medicine by MYCIN (Shortliffe, 1976). However, although a system such as MYCIN might analyze problems in microbial infection, it lacked general knowledge in anatomy and physiology which prevented a full explanation of the conditions under which its own diagnostic recommendations should not be followed. At the third level of development, a structure of scientific principles and general knowledge, together with general problem-solving methods and some domain-specific knowledge, generates the power of multi-domain problem solving in the natural sciences. The beginnings of such an integrated structure is exemplified in the FERMI system (Larkin, Reif, Carbonell, and Gugliotta, 1988).

Rationale of the FERMI Problem-Solving System

Named for the famous physicist Enrico Fermi (1901–1954), who possessed a distinctive ability to apply general principles to specific domains of physical science, FERMI (Flexible Expert Reasoner with Multi-domain Inferencing) derives its generative power from two hierarchies of knowledge, which are arranged according to their generality or scope; one hierarchy of scientific principles and one of problem-solving methods. FERMI can now solve problems in fluid pressures, electric circuits, and centroid mass, and its rationale can be extended successively to additional problem domains in the natural sciences. As applied to problems in the quantitative sciences, FERMI possesses general knowledge applicable across domains (for example, the general principle of invariance and the general principle of decomposition), specific knowledge applicable within domains (such as drops in electric potential and determination of the center of mass of a planar object), and strategic methods (for instance, the method of depth-first search, the method of breadth-first search, and the method of means–ends analysis) to control the selection and application of levels and types of knowledge and procedures.

Characteristics of FERMI

The Principle of Decomposition

A quantity such as the total pressure drop associated with the total path in a fluid can be decomposed into the pressure drop associated with each segment or the component of the path. Inversely, composition of the segmental drops can yield the total pressure drop in the path.

The decomposition principle can be summarized in the following equation:

$$Q(E) = \Sigma_i Q(E_i),$$

where $[E_i]$ is a set of entities that can be composed into the original entity E. More generally the summation might be replaced by other composition functions (e.g., multiplication, weighted addition).

The general "decomposition method" associated with this principle applies to all decomposable quantities. It specifies the following general procedure to find the value of a quantity from the values associated with its components: (1) If a quantity Q is decomposable with respect to an entity E, find a decomposition into component entities E_i such that each associated value $Q(E_i)$ is less difficult to compute than Q. (2) Compute the values $Q(E_i)$ associated with all these component entities. (3) Combine these values by using the specified combination function.

The decomposition principle and associated decomposition methods apply to functions of many types of entities. For example, decomposition applies to pressure drops or potential drops as functions of paths, to areas or centers of mass as functions of regions, and to temporal functions expressed as functions of frequency. (Larkin, Reif, Carbonell, and Gugliotta, 1988, p. 106).

The Principle of Invariance

A quantity such as the energy of a particle remains (under certain conditions) invariant with changes in the velocity and position of the particle.

The equation

$$Q(E_i) = \text{constant, for all } E_i$$

expresses the invariance principle, where E_1 and E_2 are two values of the entity E.

The following method ("comparison of invariants") is used in conjunction with the variance principle: (1) If a quantity Q invariant with respect to an entity E, select two values (E_1 and E_2) of E relevant to quantities mentioned in the problem. (2) Compute and equate the expressions Q_1 and Q_2 for the values of Q associated with E_1 and E_2. The result of this method is an equation relating quantities of interest in the problem. [For example, the energy of a particle can be expressed in terms of its position and velocity. If the particle's energy is invariant, a consideration of the particle at two different times (corresponding to different positions and velocities of the particle) yields an equation relating these positions and velocities.] (Larkin, Reif, Carbonell, and Gugliotta, 1988, pp. 106–107)

General Knowledge

FERMI's knowledge of general principles and general methods is applicable to a range of specific domains, and is encoded in general quantity and method schemas:

A general quantity schema contains pointers to one or more general methods. These pointers are inherited by all quantities related to that general quantity by any chain of isa links. Hence, the method is general in that it applies to this entire class of quantities. . . .

For example, the current implementation of FERMI has general quantity schema called "decomposable quantity." Its major slots are the following:

"/entity":

> The decomposable quantity is a function of this specified entity. It can be decomposed with respect to any decomposition of this entity into component entities.

"/combination function":

> This combination function specifies how the desired quantity can be found from the quantities associated with the individual component entities. (For example, this combination function might be scaler addition or some weighted average.)

The schemas for many specific quantities (including "pressure drop," "potential drop," and "center of mass") are connected by isa chains to the schema "decomposable quantity." Correspondingly, all of these quantities inherit a pointer to the general method schema "decomposition" which helps to decompose complex problems into simpler ones associated with component entities. . . .

The structure used for "decomposable quantity" is also used to implement "invariant quantity." A pointer to a general method for dealing with invariant quantities is included in a general quantity schema from which it is inherited by a variety of specific quantities. In this way the general method is encoded only once, but is accessible to all those quantities. (Larkin, Reif, Carbonell, and Gugliotta, 1988, pp. 109–110)

Domain Specific Knowledge Combined with General Knowledge

When general knowledge is not sufficient to solve problems, FERMI can access its domain-specific knowledge, which is stored in specific quantity schemas. Examples of problems that are solvable by FERMI's general knowledge and examples of problems that require a combination of general and domain-specific knowledge are presented below.

Method Schemas

Problem-solving methods are encoded in method schemas. FERMI's most interesting method schemas are those for the general principle of decomposition (discussed above):

The schema for the decomposition method has slots specifying the kind of control structure used (iterative decomposition or recursive decomposition) and the kinds of entities (path or region) to which the decomposition is applied.

The control structure for iterative decomposition decomposes the original entity into two subentities such that (1) at least one poses a problem simpler than the original one, and (2) neither new problem is more complex than the original one. The method then repeats (recurses) the preceding process on each subproblem until the problem is solved or the solution is unachievable because a nonsolvable subproblem cannot be further decomposed. (Larkin, Reif, Carbonell, and Gugliotta, 1988, p. 113)

Examples of FERMI's use of iterative and recursive decomposition are given below.

FERMI possesses a hierarchical organization of its specific and general knowledge and method schemas. Thus, domain-specific schemas have access to all the knowledge contained in more general schemas. The hierarchy of FERMI's quantity schemas is depicted, in part, in Figure 3.1. There are a number of advantages deriving from the inheritance structure of the schema hierarchy depicted there:

Figure 3.1
FERMI's Hierarchy of Quantities

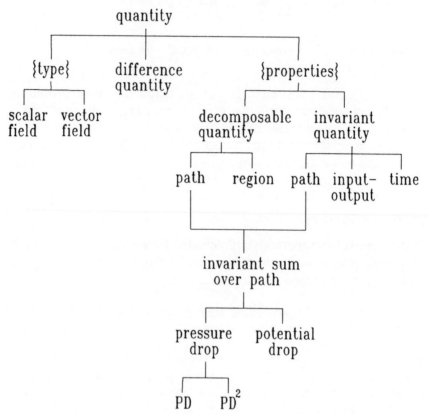

FLEXIBLE EXPERT REASONER

Source: J. H. Larkin, F. Reif, J. Carbonell, and A. Gugliotta, FERMI: A Flexible Expert Reasoner with Multi-Domain Inferencing *(Cognitive Science, 12,* 1988), p. 117. Copyright 1988 by Ablex Publishing Company. Reprinted with permission.

1. *Inheritance simplifies coding.* General knowledge needs to be encoded only once and can then be used repeatedly by a large variety of more specific schemas.

2. *Inheritance makes it easy to apply old information in new ways.* For example, electric potential drop, like pressure drop, is a difference and an invariant sum over path. The specific formulae for computing such a potential drop are, however, completely different. Nevertheless, the "potential drop" schema in [Figure 3.1] was easily added to the system after all schemas shown there had been completed. It provided only a small amount of domain-specific information about how to compute potential drops, but immediately inherited a large amount of essential information from the previously coded general schemas. As a result,

very little new programming was required to allow FERMI to apply old knowledge to a new domain.

3. *Inheritance facilitates the encoding of specific problems.* For example, a specific quantity in a problem, such as a specific pressure drop PD[1], is simply encoded as a schema "PD[1]" that is a "pressure drop." Thus, it automatically inherits all the knowledge of the quantity schema, including pointers to pullers and general methods. In addition, problem-specific knowledge (e.g., pointers to the specific points between which the particular pressure drop "PD[1]" is to be found) is encoded in the relevant slots of the particular PD[1] schema. Thus FERMI is provided with immediate access to both specific and general information.

4. *Inheritance provides an easy way to encode general principles.* Inheritance through isa links is the means whereby FERMI encodes what physical scientists call "principles." Thus the principle of conservation of energy, asserting that the energy of a system is an invariant quantity under certain conditions, is encoded by establishing an isa link between an appropriate energy schema and the knowledge associated with an invariant quantity, including a pointer to all problem-solving methods exploiting invariance. Similarly, the isa chain between "pressure drop" and "invariant sum over path" in [Figure 3.1] expresses the principle that pressure drops are path-invariant.

5. *Inheritance encourages consistency.* When a decision is made about how to encode certain knowledge (i.e., what slots to create, etc.), that decision is implemented in the most general schema to which it is applicable. Inheritance then assures that the decision is consistently implemented for all of the specific schemas connected to that general schema.

Among quantities in the physical sciences, conflicting multiple inheritances appear not to be a problem. An inheritance link between a specific and general property (e.g., between "pressure drop" and "path independent quantity") is exactly equivalent to the correct physical statement that pressure drops are path independent. Similarly, the link from "pressure drop" to "path decomposable quantity" means exactly that pressure drops are decomposable over path. Inheritance links are placed in the quantity hierarchy only when such corresponding statements are physically correct. This correctness means that the methods accessed from the general quantities do apply correctly to the specific quantities that inherit this access. "Pressure drop" is both path invariant and path decomposable, and knowledge associated with either or both may be correctly applied. (Larkin, Reif, Carbonell, and Gugliotta, 1988, pp. 118–119)

FERMI's hierarchy of method schemas is depicted in Figure 3.2. Schemas lower in the hierarchy can inherit the knowledge of more general schemas:

The method schemas contain filled "/step generator" slots with contents corresponding either to recursive, iterative or known decomposition methods. In the "iterative decomposition" schema, this slot is filled with pointers

Figure 3.2
FERMI's Hierarchy of Major Problem-Solving Methods

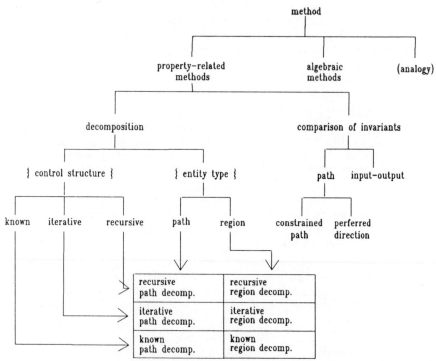

Source: J. H. Larkin, F. Reif, J. Carbonell, and A. Gugliotta, FERMI: A Flexible Expert Reasoner with Multi-Domain Inferencing (*Cognitive Science, 12,* 1988), p. 120. Copyright 1988 by Ablex Publishing Company. Reprinted with permission.

to code that specifies how to construct a first solvable problem and how then to iterate this process to generate a sequence of such solvable problems. In the "recursive decomposition" schema, this slot contains pointers to code that specifies how to subdivide a problem into two subproblems, and how then recursively to construct more such subproblems. In the "known path decomposition" the code simply identifies subproblems already present in the problem representation. The entity-type schemas contain slots with fillers specifying whether the entity of interest is a path or a region. They also contain slots with pointers to schemas providing knowledge of the details of decomposition specific either to paths or to regions.

The structure of the hierarchy, involving the invariance method for comparing invariants, is quite similar. The general "comparison of invariants" schema contains a control structure specifying how to generate equations exploiting the invariance property of a quantity. As indicated in [Figure 3.2], this control structure is then inherited by the more specific invariance methods lower in the hierarchy (e.g., by invariance with respect to changes from input to output current at a node in an electric circuit). (Larkin, Reif, Carbonell, and Gugliotta, 1988, pp. 120–121)

FERMI's Solution of Physics Problems

Example One

The following problem illustrates FERMI's use of combined general and specific knowledge to solve a problem in pressure drop:

A beaker is partly filled with water of density $p_w = 1.0$ gram/cm^3. A layer of oil, of density $p_w = 0.8$ gram/cm^3 floats on top, as shown in [Figure 3.3]. What is the pressure drop from a point A, located 2 cm below the water-oil interface, to another point B located 1 cm above the interface and 4 cm to the right of A?

This problem violates "pressure drop/computability requirements" in two ways because the points are neither in the same liquid nor located vertically one above the other. Hence, FERMI calls on the general method of path decomposition, inherited by the "pressure drop/methods" slot from "decomposable quantity." This method seeks a set of path segments that (1) collectively make up a path from A to B, and (2) individually satisfy the "pressure drop/computability requirements." The result is the set of segments A-X, X-Y, and Y-B shown in [Figure 3.3]. This step uses general knowledge. FERMI then computes a pressure drop for each of these constructed segments, and then composes them (by addition) to obtain the orig-

Figure 3.3
A Pressure-Drop Problem Requiring Both General and Domain-Specific Knowledge

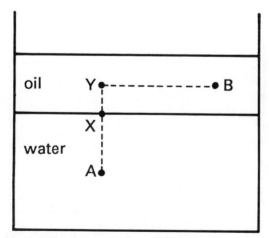

inally desired pressure drop. This step uses both the domain-specific formula for pressure drop and a general method for combining quantities with a composition function (here addition). In other words, FERMI performs the following calculation for pressure drops indicated by the symbol P:

$$P_{AB} = P_{Ax} + P_{xy} + P_{xB}$$
$$= 0 + p_wg(2) + p_cg(1)$$
$$= 0 + (1.0)(980)(2) + (0.8)(980)(1)$$
$$= 2744 \text{ dyne/cm}^3$$

Here FERMI uses the known value $g = 980$ for the gravitational acceleration. (For simplicity, the present implementation of FERMI suppresses units, assuming that all quantities are specified in terms of the fundamental units of centimeter, gram, and second.) (Larkin, Reif, Carbonell, and Gugliotta, 1988, p. 111)

Example Two

FERMI's application of its method and quantity schemas and, in particular, its application of recursive path decomposition, is illustrated in the following example:

Consider the problem of finding the pressure drop from A to B in water-filled container shown in [Figure 3.4].

Figure 3.4
Figure Illustrating a Problem Solved with Recursive Path Decomposition

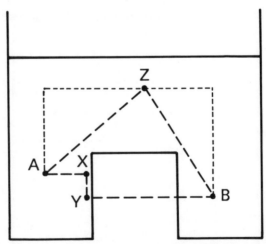

Source: J. H. Larkin, F. Reif, J. Carbonell, and A. Gugliotta, FERMI: A Flexible Expert Reasoner with Multi-Domain Inferencing (*Cognitive Science, 12,* 1988), p. 115. Copyright 1988 by Ablex Publishing Company. Reprinted with permission.

When FERMI tries to solve this problem, it successively tries to apply the available methods specified in the "pressure drop" schema. In this case, the "pressure drop/result" pullers fail because the conditions specified by "/computability requirements" are violated (i.e., intervening walls intersect the straight path from A to B). FERMI then tries to solve the problem by using "iterative path decomposition." This effort also fails for the following reasons: FERMI first constructs the path segments A-X and X-Y shown in [Figure 3.4], thereby moving closer to B and satisfying all computability requirements. But when FERMI tries to iterate the process, considering the remaining path Y-B, it cannot find a path segment that begins as Y moves closer to B, and satisfies the "pressure drop/computability requirements."

At this point, FERMI tries the method of "recursive path decomposition," the second general method schema associated with "pressure drop." This method tries to find a point Z satisfying the following conditions: (1) At least one of the new paths A-Z and Z-B violate fewer of the computability requirements than the original path A-B, and (2) neither path violates more computability requirements than the original path. The means for generating a path which does not violate a particular computability requirement is stored with the computability requirement itself. In this case the "in container" requirement stores the following method: Start at the center of the line joining the two points of interest, A and B. Move along the perpendicular bisector of this line until reaching a point Z for which AZ and BZ do not violate the incontainer restruction. If point Z itself moves outside the container, then move in the opposite direction. The result is the point Z shown in [Figure 3.4]. Note that the original path A-B violated all three computability requirements, i.e., that it should lie in a region of homogeneous liquid density, that it should not intersect any walls, and that it should be along a preferred direction (vertical or horizontal). By contrast, each of the new paths A-Z and Z-B violates only the single computability requirement that it should be along a preferred direction.

The problem solution is completed as discussed earlier by applying domain-specific knowledge to the simple vertical and horizontal paths. (Larkin, Reif, Carbonell, and Gugliotta, 1988, pp. 114–115).

Example Three

FERMI solves the following problem by means of iterative region decomposition:

Consider finding the center of mass of the two-dimensional metal object [weather vane] shown in [Figure 3.5].

As always, FERMI starts its work by trying direct domain-specific methods encoded as pullers. Here the "center of mass" schema contains the following method, encoded in the puller of the "/result" slot and in the

"/computability requirements" slot: If a rectangular object is aligned parallel to the x and y axes, with two parallel sides located at x_1 and x_2 and the other two parallel sides at y_1 and y_2, the center-of-mass coordinates x_c and y_c are found by computing the respective averages of these positions.

Direct application of the puller fails in this case because the weather vane is not rectangular in shape. Then FERMI tries to apply iterative decomposition because the "center of mass/methods" slot contains a pointer to "iterative region decomposition." To do this, FERMI starts at an arbitrary corner of the weather vane, say corner A in [Figure 3.5], and constructs a region satisfying the following requirements: (1) The region satisfies the "center of mass/computability requirements" of being a rectangle. (2) The remaining region should be as small as possible, i.e., the chosen rectangle should be as large as possible. The chosen rectangular region is the rectangle ABCD indicated in [Figure 3.5].

The "region decomposition/done test" then determines that the computability requirements are satisfied by the three remaining rectangular regions. (Note that this "/done test," unlike that used for path decomposition, must be able to cope with multiple remaining regions.) FERMI then calculates the centers of mass for all four regions, and combines them using the "center of mass/composition function" (average position weighted by mass). (Larkin, Reif, Carbonell, and Gugliotta, 1988, pp. 115–116)

Example Four

In the following example, FERMI combines its knowledge and depth-first search to solve a complex problem:

Figure 3.5
A Problem Solved with Iterative Region Decomposition

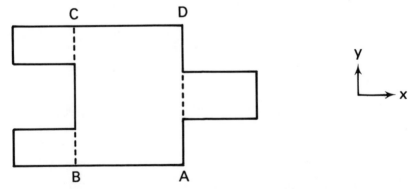

The problem is that of finding the current I_0 in [Figure 3.6a]. Figure [3.6b] shows a slightly simplified goal tree constructed from the trace of FERMI's solution. . . .

As FERMI applies its domain-specific methods and physical-science methods to this problem, it constructs either single subgoals or sets of subgoals. A subgoal set is either an AND set, (indicated by double arcs in [Figure 3.6a]), or an OR set, (indicated by single arcs). To satisfy the parent goal, all of an AND set must be satisfied, but just one of an OR set must be satisfied.

FERMI generates and searches the tree in [Figure 3.6b] left-to-right depth-first (a very general weak method). In particular, attempts to satisfy (left to right) each new node in a newly-generated subgoal set. An x through the line leading to the node indicates that FERMI could neither satisfy that node (through lookup or pullers) nor could it generate any new subgoals (with methods). That node is therefore a failure and FERMI backs up to the first available OR set above the failure, and tries the next goal in that set. Each x is labeled with a number, keyed at the bottom of [Figure 3.6b] to a list of reasons for possible failures.

Three kinds of goal nodes appear in [Figure 3.6b]. The goal to find the value of a single quantity (e.g., I_0, V_1) is represented by that quantity. Goals to apply a method appear as italicized phrases (e.g., I-O invariance for input-output invariance). These are always subgoals of quantity goals. An equation in [Figure 3.6b] indicates a goal to instantiate that equation and to solve

Figure 3.6a
Circuit Diagram for a Problem Requiring Application of Domain-Specific Knowledge, Physical-Science Methods, and Weak Search Methods

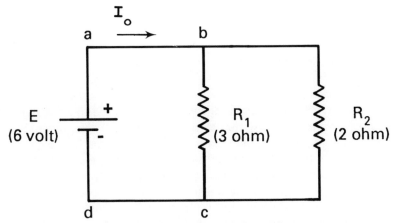

Source: J. H. Larkin, F. Reif, J. Carbonell, and A. Gugliotta, FERMI: A Flexible Expert Reasoner with Multi-Domain Inferencing (*Cognitive Science, 12,* 1988), p. 123. Copyright 1988 by Ablex Publishing Company. Reprinted with permission.

Figure 3.6b
Goal Tree for FERMI's Solution to the Problem

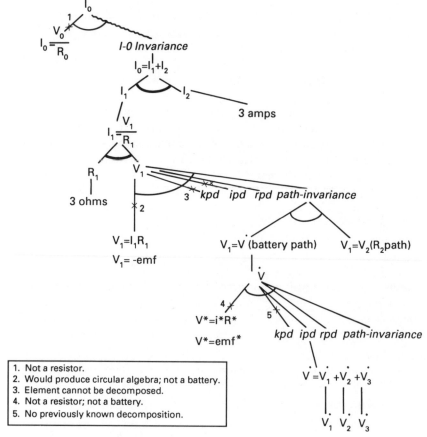

1. Not a resistor.
2. Would produce circular algebra; not a battery.
3. Element cannot be decomposed.
4. Not a resistor; not a battery.
5. No previously known decomposition.

Source: J. H. Larkin, F. Reif, J. Carbonell, and A. Gugliotta, FERMI: A Flexible Expert Reasoner with Multi-Domain Inferencing (*Cognitive Science, 12,* 1988), p. 124. Copyright 1988 by Ablex Publishing Company. Reprinted with permission.

it for the first quantity appearing above it in the tree. Equation goals arise either from application of the method above it, or from application of a puller (indicated by a P) on the arc leading to the equation.

Briefly, this solution proceeds as follows: The puller ($I = V/R$) associated with I_0 fails because the resistance associated with a wire is zero. Therefore the single method associated with current (input–output invariance) is invoked to generate the equation $I_0 = I_1 + I_2$. Instantiating this equation requires values for both of the new quantities, that is an AND subgoal to find I_1 and I_2. The work to find I_1 and I_2 is identical, and [Figure 3.6b] shows only that for I_1, with the result (3 amps) given for I_2. (The dotted line indicates omitted work.) The puller associated with the current I_1 generates the goal to instantiate the equation $I_1 = V_1/R_1$, with the following AND subgoal set of finding values for V_1 and R_1. Working left to right, FERMI considers V_1 first. (R_1 is subsequently evaluated as 3 ohms by lookup.) The two pullers for potential drop both fail here. In the first, $V_1 = I_1 R_2$, I_1 has already been "visited" higher on the tree and introducing it here would lead to circular algebra. The second puller ($V = -$ emf) fails because the element is not a battery.

FERMI then creates an OR set of subgoals to apply methods associated with potential drop. The first three (known, iterative, and recursive path decomposition) fail because the element here cannot be composed. The final method, path invariance, generates two equations, reflecting that V_1 is equal to the potential drop (V_2) along the path through resistor 2 and V_1 is also equal to the potential drop (V^*) along the path through the battery. Both pullers fail to apply to V^* because this path is neither a resistor nor a battery, but a composite of two wires (resistors with zero resistance) and a battery. Applying sequentially the four methods associated with V^*, known-path-decomposition (kpd) fails because the path has not been decomposed, but iterative path decomposition succeeds in breaking the path into the wires (paths 1* and 3*) and the battery (path 2*). Pullers yield the indicated values for each of the associated potential drops. (The usual puller steps are omitted here from [Figure 3.6b], as indicated by dotted lines.)

Now FERMI applies further knowledge from its methods as it works back up the successful branches of its tree, combining values according to combination functions in the methods. The potential drop V^*, and hence V_1, is 0 + 6 + 0, or 6 volts. The puller equation $I_1 = V_1 + R_1$ combines the values 6 volts and 3 ohms to yield $I_1 = 2$ amps. The value $I_z = 3$ amps (found by a process exactly analogous to that used for I_1) is added to $I_1 = 2$ amps by input–output invariance to yield the desired value 5 amps. (Larkin, Reif, Carbonell, and Gugliotta, 1988, pp. 123–125)

The developers of FERMI summarize its present abilities to solve problems in the natural sciences as follows:

Problems about pressures in liquids. FERMI can find the pressure difference between any two points in one or more liquids at rest, even when there are several distinct layers of such liquids, and even if these liquids are in a container whose walls interrupt a direct straight line connecting the points of interest.
Problems about centers of mass. FERMI can find the center of mass of any planar object which is rectangular or decomposable into rectangular parts.
Problems about electric circuits. FERMI can find time-independent po-

tential drops or currents in electric circuits consisting of any small number of wires, resistors, and batteries interconnected in various ways.

FERMI can also now apply invariance of energy to relate the mass and speeds of a satellite or a falling object at two different locations. (Larkin, Reif, Carbonell, and Gugliotta, 1988, p. 126)

Future Development of FERMI

The most interesting future development planned for FERMI is the extension of the general principles of decomposition and invariance to additional domains in the physical sciences and the incorporation of new general principles. Table 3.1 presents an impressive range of domains to which (with appropriately added specific-domain knowledge) the principle of decomposition can be extended. Table 3.2 presents a description of the domains to which the principle of invariance can be extended.

A new general principle of "fixed value constraints" could, when developed, augment FERMI's capacity as a problem solver in the physical sciences. In particular, the constraint that mathematical expressions for physical concepts must have a fixed value equal to zero is pervasive in many domains of physics:

For example, in the domain of mechanics, an object remains in equilibrium (without accelerating) if the total force F exerted on the object by all other interacting objects satisfies the constraint that $F = 0$. Similarly, the domain of electricity, an isolated electrically neutral object must have a total charge Q which satisfies at all times the charge-conservation principle that $Q = 0$. (Larkin, Reif, Carbonell, and Gugliotta, 1988, p. 127)

Commentary

FERMI has achieved a certain generality and flexibility of application due to its organizational structure and its use of general principles such as decomposition and invariance. As discussed in the beginning of this section, the use of general principles is both an advance over systems that possessed only domain-specific knowledge and a useful modelling of the approach to problems for which its namesake Enrico Fermi was well known. However, the structure of knowledge in an artificial intelligence system such as that of FERMI imposes limits on flexibility. Where Enrico Fermi was free to select

Table 3.1
Domains with Important Quantities That Are Decomposable (shown in italics)

Liquids at rest	*Pressure drop* between any two points
Electric circuits	The *Potential drop* between any two points
Geometry	*Length* of a line, *area* of a surface, *volume* of a region
Mechanics	*Mass* of an object, *center of mass* of an object, the *force*, exerted on an object by other interacting objects
Electricity and magnetism	*Electric field, magnetic field, electric and magnetic potentials*
Heat and thermodynamics	*Internal energy* of any system, *entropy* of any system
Chemistry	*Molecular weight, reaction rate*, several reacting chemical species
Waves	*Wave disturbance*, due to several waves present simultaneously

Source: J. H. Larkin, F. Reif, J. Carbonell, and A. Gugliotta, FERMI: A Flexible Expert Reasoner with Multi-Domain Inferencing (*Cognitive Science, 12,* 1988), p. 126.

Table 3.2
Four Kinds of Invariance

Path	Pressure and potential drop are invariant under changes in path. Any path may be used to calculate them
Input-Output Invariance	Steady-state flow rates of charge, mass; quantities unchanging in the course of time. (Such quantites obey a "conservation principle" and include momentum, angular momentum, energy.)
Spatial	Rotated through a 90^0 angle or 180^0 angle. Many quantities can often be determined for such symmetries.

Source: J. H. Larkin, F. Reif, J. Carbonell, and A. Gugliotta, FERMI: A Flexible Expert Reasoner with Multi-Domain Inferencing (*Cognitive Science, 12,* 1988), p. 127.

general principles and specific knowledge and to permute and combine these knowledge sources in an adaptive way, the FERMI system unadaptively follows its fixed sequenced procedures. FERMI represents a third level of development in the increasing sophistication of expert systems (see section above on the general logic of problem-solving systems); it remains to be seen whether there is an inherent quality in artificial intelligence systems that forever proscribes a fourth level of development characterized by adaptive ingenuity and the intelligent discernment of the essential nature of a problem.

ARTIFICIAL INTELLIGENCE AND MEDICAL PROBLEM SOLVING

The General Logic of Medical Problem Solving

In recent years, research in cognitive science has attempted to use the logic of information-processing systems to model the diagnostic logic of expert physicians. The concepts of production rules (if–then relationships) and of forward or backward chaining (the sequential direction of reasoning) are used to model the physician's knowledge and reasoning process. A general goal of this research is to establish the logical processes and knowledge constituents that distinguish expert from inexpert physicians and accurate from inaccurate diagnoses. A representative example of such cognitive research will be discussed (Patel and Groen, 1986).

The Techniques of Propositional Analysis

V. L. Patel and G. J. Groen (1986) were interested in determining the logical processes of medical problem solving with a high degree of explicitness and precision. To obtain explicitness, they conducted an experiment in which seven cardiologists, following their reading of a patient's case, were requested to write down as much as they could recall of the case, and then were requested to write down the pathophysiological knowledge involved in their explanation of the case. To obtain precision, the patient's case, the recall protocols, and the pathophysiological protocols were subjected to the techniques of propositional analysis. Application of propositional analysis results in the detection of the propositions in a text and a determination of relationships among the detected proposition.

In the present study we are primarily concerned with the processes used by our experts in generating a diagnostic explanation. Our basic strategy is to map the propositions in the text and the recall protocol onto those in the pathophysiology protocol. The propositional analysis of the text . . . begins with a division of the text into segments on the basis of Winograd's (1972) classification of discourse into major and secondary clauses. For example, consider the following sentence:

Urinanalysis showed numerous red cells, but there were no red cell casts.

Winograd's system of clausal analysis is used to determine the following two clausal segments: a declarative major clause and a bound adjunct. The bound adjunct is the only secondary clause in Winograd's system that we consider as a separate segment. The result is two segments, consisting of a major clause: (1) Urinanalysis showed numerous red cells and a secondary bound adjunct; (2) but there were no red cell casts. We then perform a propositional analysis of each segment. The conceptual structures encoded in the first segment are the following three propositions:

1.0	CAU	[URINALYSIS][1.1];
1.1	SHOW	THM: 1.2 = TNS:PAST:ATT:RED;
1.2	CELLS (NUM: NUMEROUS)	

Encoded in the second segment is the following proposition:

2.0	CASTS (NUM:NULL(N))	ATT:CELL;
2.1	CELL	ATT: RED;

. . . Each proposition is formally an n-place relation. It is identified by a head element which is followed by a list of its labelled arguments, separated by commas. The head element may be an action, an object, or a relation which connects propositions (e.g., CAU, a causal relation; or COND, a conditional relation). We will call the relations which connect propositions *linking propositions*. They are extremely important for our purposes because, as we shall see, they can be used to define rules. There are only 10 propositions of this type in the text, 8 of which are causal relations (CAU), one is an equivalence relation (EQUI), and the remaining one refers to temporal ordering (ORD:TEM).

It should be emphasized that the names of linking propositions are labels whose meaning may vary depending on the context. Thus, a label such as CAU or COND does not necessarily refer to a "cause" or "condition" in the logical or semantic sense. In the previous example, CAU refers to a clinical procedure. In much of our analysis to follow, CAU refers to some statement regarding the functioning of the underlying pathophysiology. This is a natural consequence of the fact that propositional analysis is intended as a domain-independent representational language. (Patel and Groen, 1986, pp. 97–98)

A Case of Bacterial Endocarditis

The cardiologists in the research study were given two and a half minutes to study the medical history of a patient. The case history is presented here:

Text: Bacterial Endocarditis

This 27 year old unemployed male was admitted to the emergency room with the complaint of shaking chills and fever of four days' duration. He took his own temperature and it was recorded at 40°C on the morning of his admission. The fever and chills were accompanied by sweating and a feeling of prostration. He also complained of some shortness of breath when he tried to climb the two flights of stairs in his apartment. Functional inquiry revealed a transient loss of vision in his right eye which lasted approximately 45 s on the day before his admission to the emergency ward.

Physical examination revealed a toxic looking young man who was having a rigor. His temperature was 41°C, pulse 120, BP 110/40. Mucus membranes were pink. Examination of his limbs showed puncture wounds in his left antecubital fossa. The patient volunteered that he had been bitten by a cat at a friend's house about a week before admission. There were no other skin findings. Examination of the cardiovascular system showed no jugular venous distention, pulse was 120 per minute, regular, equal, and synchronous. The pulse was also noted to be collapsing. The apex beat was not displaced. Auscultation of his heart revealed a 2/6 early diastolic murmur in the aortic area and funduscopy revealed a flame shaped hemorrhage in the left eye. There was no splenomegaly. Urinalysis showed numerous red cells but there were no red cell casts. (Patel and Groen, 1986, p. 97)

Cardiologists Recall Protocol of the Case

Following their study of the text of the case, the text was removed and the cardiologists were requested to reproduce the text in writing in maximum detail. The recall protocol produced by one cardiologist is presented here:

Expert Recall Protocol Number 5

THIS (UNEMPLOYED) 27-YEAR-OLD MALE PRESENTED TO THE EMERGENCY ROOM WITH HISTORY OF FEVER OF 40°C AND SHAKING CHILLS OF 4 DAYS DURATION. HE ALSO COMPLAINED OF SHORTNESS OF BREATH (SOB) WHILE GOING UP STAIRS. HE RECALLED HAVING BEEN BIT BY A FRIEND'S CAT THE WEEK BE-

FORE. HE ALSO HAD A TRANSIENT LOSS OF VISION IN HIS RIGHT EYE THE DAY PRIOR TO ADMISSION.

HE HAD A BLOOD PRESSURE OF 110/40 AND COLLAPSING PULSE. HIS HEART RATE WAS ELEVATED. HE HAD PUNCTURE WOUNDS IN THE LEFT ANTECUBITAL FOSSA AND NO OTHER SKIN FINDINGS. FUNDOSCOPIC EXAMINATION REVEALED A FLAME SHAPED HEMORRHAGE. HIS JVP WAS NOT INCREASED. HIS APEX WAS NOT DISPLACED. HE HAD AN EARLY DIASTOLIC MURMUR AT THE LEFT STOMACH BORDER. HIS SPLEEN WAS NOT ENLARGED. URINALYSIS SHOWED CASTS WHICH I BELIEVE WERE GRANULAR. (Patel and Groen, 1986, p. 99)

The recall is essentially a compact version of the text in which there are two main features of interest. First, there are only two links, both of which are causal relations, compared to eight in the text. Second, the patient's attribution of his skin punctures to a "cat bite" is moved from the middle of the text to the beginning of the protocol. This is consistent with the notion that our expert is making use of a "standard schema" which is extensively taught at medical school. It divides a case description into three components: characterization of patient, history, and physical examination. Thus, the information about the cat bite moves from the physical examination component into the history, where it belongs from this point of view. This is the only evidence of a constructive process in the entire recall protocol. Otherwise, it is a verbatim summary with no essential information omitted. (Patel and Groen, 1986, p. 99)

Cardiologists' Pathophysiological Explanation of the Case

Following their completion of recall protocols, the cardiologist produced written protocols that contain their explanation of the pathophysiological basis of the case and their diagnosis. The pathophysiological explanation of one cardiologist is presented here:

Expert Pathophysiology Protocol Number 5

THE IMPORTANT POINTS ARE THE ACUTE ONSET OF CHILLS AND FEVER IN A YOUNG MALE WITH PUNCTURE WOUNDS IN THE LEFT ANTECUBITAL FOSSA INDICATING HIGH PROBABILITY OF DRUG ABUSE AND THEREFORE SUSCEPTIBLE TO ENDOCARDITIS.

THE HISTORY OF TRANSIENT BLINDNESS IN ONE EYE SUPPORTS AN EMBOLIC PHENOMENA FOR A LEFT VALVULAR VEGI-

TATION. THE SHORTNESS OF BREATH (SOB) ON EXERTION AND
THE EARLY DIASTOLIC MURMUR PLUS WIDE PULSE PRESSURE
SUPPORT AORTIC INSUFFICIENCY AND THUS AORTIC VALVE EN-
DOCARDITIS. THE NORMAL SPLEEN SIZE INDICATES A MORE
ACUTE PROCESS. THE URINARY FINDINGS SUPPORT RENAL EM-
BOLI. THE HISTORY OF BEING SCRATCHED BY A CAT RAISES
THE DIFFERENTIAL DIAGNOSIS OF CAT SCRATCH FEVER, BUT
THERE ARE NO OTHER SUPPORTING FINDINGS. (Patel and Groen,
1986, p. 99)

In contrast [to the recall protocol], the explanation of the underlying pathophysiology seems quite different, bearing a much more remote relation to
the original text. . . . The chief difference is that there are once again many
linking propositions. In contrast to the two in the recall protocol, there are
now nine. Although this is approximately the same as in the text, there are
considerably fewer propositions in the pathophysiology protocol (41 versus
87) so the proposition of linking propositions is far greater. Seven of the
linking propositions are causal (most involve reverse causality indicated by
SUPPORTS). One is a condition (COND) and the other is an identity relation (IDEN). They are quite different from the linking propositions in the
text, most of which say that if a certain physical examination procedure is
undertaken then a certain pattern of findings is obtained. Most of those in
the pathophysiology protocol say that a certain pattern of findings supports
the notion of some causal mechanism or vice versa. (Patel and Groen, 1986,
pp. 99–100)

Causal Roles and Expert Knowledge

In order to ascertain the canonical or basic knowledge necessary to
produce a pathophysiological protocol of the type shown in Table
3.4, a cardiologist, not involved in the experiment, was requested to
state the relevant canonical knowledge of endocarditis in the form of
causal rules. Figure 3.7 represents the canonical knowledge necessary
to reach the diagnosis of acute bacterial endocarditis with aortic insufficiency.

The rules in this diagram [Figure 3.7] are represented as causal rules, because this kind of information was simpler to obtain from our independent
expert. It is important to note, however, that such causal rules can be reversed into conditions, and hence represent reasoning of the type the subject
in the preceding section was using. This diagram [Figure 3.7] therefore provides a general framework that allows forward or backward reasoning depending on the direction on which the rules are applied. It should be noted,

Figure 3.7
Canonical Frame for Acute Bacterial Endocarditis (ABE) with Aortic Insufficiency

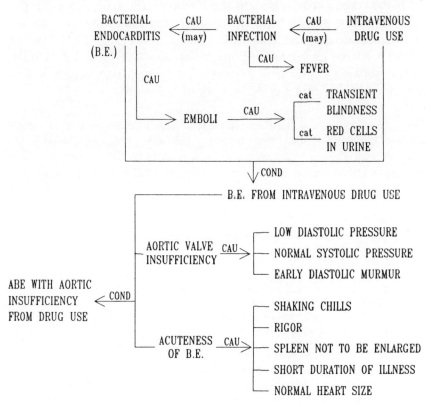

CAU: Casual Relation

COND: Conditional Relation

Source: V. L. Patel and G. J. Groen, Knowledge Based Solution Strategies in Medical Reasoning (*Cognitive Science, 10,* 1986), p. 103. Copyright 1986 by Ablex Publishing Company. Reprinted with permission.

however, that the COND rules leading to the actual diagnosis cannot be reversed in this fashion.

For example, the causal rule "if infection, then fever" implies the conditional rule "if fever, then infection." On the other hand, the purely conditional rule "if intravenous drug use, then bacterial infection" cannot be reversed, because bacterial infection clearly does not indicate intravenous drug use. (Patel and Groen, 1986, p. 104)

Accuracy of Diagnosis and Production Rules

Of the seven cardiologists in the research study, four reached the accurate diagnosis. In order to compare the reasoning of accurate and inaccurate diagnosticians, their causal networks (such as that in Figure 3.7) were converted to production rules (see Table 3.3). Unlike causal networks, production rules, consisting of antecedents and consequents, indicate a directionality of reasoning.

The antecedents and consequents (which determine the direction in which the rules are being applied) were directly obtained by matching linking propositions with elements of the canonical frame from the protocols of the three subjects who generated accurate diagnoses. All of these rules are in a

Table 3.3
Production Rules That Yield an Accurate Diagnosis

Production Rule (#)	Antecedent (if)	Consequence (then)
1	Puncture wounds and young unemployed male	Intravenous drug use
2	Intravenous drug use	Bacterial infection
3	Bacterial infection and emboli	Bacterial endocarditis
4	Fever	Bacterial infection
5	Transient blindness	Emboli
6	Red blood cells in urine	Emboli
7	Intravenous drug use and bacterial endocarditis	Bacterial endocarditis from intravenous drug use
8	Low diastolic pressure and normal systolic pressure	Aortic valve insufficiency
9	Early diastolic murmur	Aortic valve insufficiency
10	Shaking chills and bacterial endocarditis	Acuteness of bacterial endocarditis
11	Rigor and bacterial endocarditis	Acuteness of bacterial endocarditis
12	Normal spleen and bacterial endocarditis	Acuteness of bacterial endocarditis
13	Short duration of illness and bacterial endocarditis	Acuteness of bacterial endocarditis
14	Normal heart size and bacterial endocarditis	Acuteness of bacterial endocarditis
15	Bacterial endocarditis from intravenous drug use, aortic valve insufficiency, and acuteness of bacterial endocarditis	Acute bacterial endocarditis with aortic insufficiency from drug use.

Source: V. L. Patel and G. J. Groen, Knowledge Based Solution Strategies in Medical Reasoning (*Cognitive Science, 10,* 1986), p. 104.

forward direction toward the diagnosis. There is no instance of backtracking. This implies that all four subjects were using pure forward reasoning. In fact, an identical analysis to that performed for the single subject in the preceding section indicates an identical pattern for the three remaining subjects, with the relevant propositions of the recall protocols being used as input to the frames derived from the pathophysiology protocols.

Some of these rules were also used by the three subjects who generated inaccurate diagnoses. The use made by all subjects of these rules is shown in [Table 3.4]. This table indicates that the critical rules for an accurate diagnosis are Rule 2 (IF intravenous drug use, THEN bacterial infection), and Rule 9 (IF early diastolic murmur, THEN aortic insufficiency). None of the subjects who generated an inaccurate diagnosis used these rules, whereas they were all subjects who generated an accurate diagnosis.

The subject who generated inaccurate diagnosis made use of additional rules. These are of two kinds: irrelevant rules and backward chaining rules. This is shown . . . [by the] pathophysiology protocol of subject 6, who gave a diagnosis of subacute aortic insufficiency. It contains an irrelevant branch that deals with a perceived lack of severity of the illness rather than linking "no cardiomegaly" to signs of acuteness. Most interesting, however, is the fact that the reasoning is mainly top-down. It begins with a general hypothesis regarding bacteremia and works backward to the text-based knowledge.

Table 3.4
Subjects' Use of Production Rules That Yield an Accurate Diagnosis

Production Rule (#)	Subjects (#) with Accurate Diagnosis				Subject (#) with Inaccurate Diagnosis		
	2	3	4	5	1	6	7
1	X	X		X			
2	X	X	X	X			
3	X		X	X	X		X
4		X	X	X	X	X	
5	X	X	X	X	X	X	X
6	X	X	X	X	X	X	
7	X		X	X	X		X
8	X		X	X	X		
9	X	X	X	X			
10			X	X		X	
11		X					
12				X			
13		X					
14	X						
15	X	X		X			

Source: V. L. Patel and G. J. Groen, Knowledge Based Solution Strategies in Medical Reasoning (*Cognitive Science, 10,* 1986), p. 105.

This use of backward reasoning is also found in the other two subjects whose diagnoses were inaccurate, although the pattern emerges most clearly with the present subject. (Patel and Groen, 1986, pp. 105–106)

Commentary

In the research of Patel and Groen (1986), expert cardiologists used forward reasoning and canonical knowledge organized as production rules to solve a complex problem in medical diagnosis. It is interesting that experts in domains beyond medicine use similar strategies of problem solving: from experts solving problems in physics (Larkin, McDermott, Simon, and Simon, 1980) to experts solving problems in chess (Chase and Simon, 1973). The broad generality of these research findings lends support to the theory of problem solving processes developed by H. A. Simon and G. Lea (1974). Simon and Lea's theory has been extended to the investigation of the nature of scientific discovery (see Chapter 4).

FOUR

Scientific Discovery and Its Cognitive Processes

In the first section of this chapter, the general logic of computational theories of scientific discovery is discussed. The computational exploration of the scientific discovery process is exemplified by the KEKADA artificial intelligence program. Based on the records of Hans Krebs's discovery or the ornithine effect, KEKADA program was constructed to simulate Krebs's cognitive processes, including his knowledge of biochemistry, hypothesis formation, and experimental procedures that led to discovery of the nature of the urea cycle. KEKADA's heuristics and control structure are described, and a detailed log of its scientific behavior is given. A comparison between KEKADA and Krebs reveals only minor differences. KEKADA's rediscovery of the ornithine effect is analyzed both as a simulation of Krebs's discovery and as a computational model of scientific discovery processes in general. The section concludes with a discussion of whether artificial intelligence approaches can be extended to simulate aspects of scientific discovery that represent the theoretical foundations of science.

In the second section of the chapter, the cognitive processes involved in scientific discovery are discussed in the context of a laboratory study and a model of scientific discovery as dual search. Experimental subjects were presented with the problem of discovering the nature of an advanced electronic device. Experimental proto-

cols reveal differential styles of discovery including the style of the
Theorist and the style of the Experimenter. The cognitive styles are
modelled and discussed in terms of a theory of scientific discovery as
search through two spaces: a hypothesis space and an experiment
space. The dual search theory provides a detailed description of the
pathways to discovery in the laboratory task. The section concludes
with an examination of two problems: the problem of whether the
theory can be generalized to scientific projects more complex than
that of the laboratory task, and the problem of how the theory can be
extended beyond its present descriptive level to an explanatory level of
the nature of the conditions that control the emergence of significant
scientific insights.

ARTIFICIAL INTELLIGENCE AND THE PROCESSES OF SCIENTIFIC DISCOVERY

The General Logic of Computational Theories of Scientific Discovery

The general logic of computational theories of scientific discovery
includes the assumption that the creative processes of scientific discovery are knowable and definable, the assumption that they represent subsets of general strategies of problem solving, the assumption
that they can be modelled by the standard heuristics of problem-
solving computational systems, and the assumption that scientific
discovery systems can not only replicate discovery processes and
products, but can also make independent and original discoveries.
Each of these assumptions will now be briefly discussed.

The assumption that creative and discovery processes are not un-
knowable or undefinable is in conflict with the prevalent and ancient
belief that human creativity is mysterious and beyond the ken of science. Creativity, whether artistic, literary, musical, philosophical,
mathematical, or scientific, was a gift from capricious muses, a special blessing from God, the crystallization of unconscious dynamics
in a neurotic personality, an inexplicable and sudden inspiration (sic,
spirit), or the intuitive insight that illumines, as if by magic, the nature of the solution to a puzzle, problem, or paradox.

The assumption that the inductive and deductive logics of scientific discovery can be mapped as sets of mechanistic problem-solving
heuristics may be unacceptable, as it appears to deny or foreshorten
the significance of the human qualities of curiosity about a problem,

interest in a phenomenon, disappointment in an experimental outcome, surprise in the face of an unexpected scientific result, frustration over failure, and elation in response to minor successes that give encouragement to the continuation of a difficult and challenging scientific enterprise. The assumption that a mechanism is necessary and sufficient appears to be unacceptable because it denies exclusivity of intellect to humans and denies the necessity of nonintellective processes.

The assumption that computer programs can replicate scientific and mathematical discoveries has received some justification. Lenat's Automatic Mathematician (AM) program (Davis and Lenat, 1980) discovered the fundamental theorem of arithmetic and the concept of prime numbers. Langley's BACON.3 program (Langley, Simon, Bradshaw, and Zytkow, 1987) rediscovered Kepler's laws of planetary motion, Galileo's laws of acceleration, Georg Ohm's laws of electricity, and the ideal gas laws. Table 4.1 presents the heuristics used by AM to discover prime numbers, and Table 4.2 presents equations for the physical laws discovered by BACON.3.

The assumption that computer programs can make independent and original scientific discoveries has received some support. The Meta-DENDRAL program (Buchanan and Feigenbaum, 1978) has made discoveries in chemistry that were considered sufficiently significant to be published in a prestigious scientific journal.

These programs demonstrate the power of mechanistic problem

Table 4.1
Equations Discovered by BACON.3

Ideal gas law	$pV/nT = K_1$
Kepler's third law	$d^3 [(a - k_2)/t]^2 = k_3$
Coulomb's law	$Fd^2/q_1 q_2 = k_4$
Galileo's laws	$dP^2/Lt^2 = k_5$
Ohm's law	$D^2 T/(LI + k_6 D^2 I) = k_7$

Source: P. Langley, Data-Driven Discovery of Physical Laws *(Cognitive Science, 5,* 1981), p. 50

Table 4.2
The PRIMES Concept Produced by AM

NAME: *Prime Numbers*
DEFINITIONS:
   ORIGIN: *Number-of-divisors-of(x)* = 2
   PREDICATE-CALCULUS: *Prime(x)<=>($\forall z$) |x=>(z = 1 $\otimes$ z = x))*
   ITERATIVE: (*for x > 1):For i from 2 to $\sqrt{x}$,i)(x*
EXAMPLES: 2,3,5,7,11,13,17
   BOUNDARY: 2,3
   BOUNDARY-FAILURES: 0,1
   FAILURES: 12
GENERALIZATIONS: *Number, numbers with an even number of divisors*
SPECIALIZATIONS: *Odd primes, prime pairs, prime uniquely addables*
CONJECS: *Unique factorization, Goldbach's conjecture, extrema of number-of-divisors-of*
INTUS: *A metaphor to the effect that primes are the building blocks of all numbers*
ANALOGIES:
   Maximally divisible numbers are converse extremes of number-of-divisors-of
   Factor a nonsimple group into simple groups.
INTEREST: *Conjectures tying primes to times, to divisors of, to related operations*
WORTH: 800

Source: Elaine Rich, *Artificial Intelligence* (New York: McGraw-Hill, 1983), p. 376.

solving. However, they were not designed to illumine or precisely model the nature of the scientist's creative processes. For example, BACON.3 rediscovered Kepler's laws of the solar system by applying general heuristics for relating variables to data presented to it, but unlike Johannes Kepler, BACON.3 did not construct and reconstruct hypotheses, explanations, and theories. Similarly, BACON.3 was provided with data from which it constructed the equations for Coulomb's laws, but unlike Charles Coulomb, it did not conduct the complex experimentation and theorizing that culminated in the collected data.

In order to advance the computational theory of scientific discovery, it is necessary to develop programs that can model the scientist's experimental concepts and procedures. The KEKADA program (Kulkarni and Simon, 1988) was developed to model the creative processes of Hans Krebs, who made important discoveries in biochemistry.

Kreb's Discovery of the Ornithine Effect

In 1932, Hans Krebs discovered by means of systematic experimentation the metabolic cycle and biochemical events involved in the liver's synthesis of urea. The discovery was highly significant in its own right, and as a model of biochemical metabolic theory it has been characterized by J. S. Fruton as "a new stage in the development of biochemical thought" (1972, p. 95). A highly detailed reconstruction of the experimental and conceptual steps by which Krebs made his discovery was achieved by F. L. Holmes (1980) on the basis of interviews with Krebs and the examination of Krebs's meticulous laboratory logs of his ongoing experiments. Holmes's description of the processes of Krebs's scientific discovery was used by D. Kulkarni and H. A. Simon (1988) to develop KEKADA, a program that would duplicate those processes and contribute to a computational theory of scientific discovery.

Before discussing KEKADA and the quality of its simulation of the processes by which Krebs made his discoveries, a brief summary of Holmes's (1980) account of those discoveries will be given.

The problem that Krebs attacked, to discover how urea was synthesized in living mammals from the decomposition products of proteins, had been investigated extensively for many years with very limited success. The methods used in Krebs' discovery, and the general nature of the catalytic process discovered, served as prototypes for much subsequent research and theory on metabolic phenomena. . . .

Course of Krebs' Research

The account of Krebs' research can be divided conveniently into three major segments: the first from July 26, 1931 to November 15, when the effects of ornithine were first noticed; the second from November 15 until about January 14, 1932, when evidence indicated that the effect was quite specific to ornithine; the third from January 14 to April 13, when Krebs was sufficiently convinced that he had discovered the synthesis mechanism to send off a paper for publication. Thus, the critical phenomenon that led to the solution of the problem was detected after about three and a half months of work, while interpreting the new phenomenon and testing the theory required another five months.

1. *The ornithine effect.* Krebs began with the idea of using the tissue-slice method, a technique he had acquired in Otto Warburg's laboratory, to study urea synthesis. He tested the efficacy of various amino acids in producing urea, with generally negative results. When he carried out the experiment with ornithine (one of the less common amino acids) and ammonia, unexpectedly large amounts of urea were produced. He then focused on the ornithine effect.

2. *Determination of scope.* Krebs next followed a standard strategy: If a given

compound exerts a particular action, check whether derivatives of that compound have a similar action. Thus, he carried out tests on some ornithine derivatives and substances similar to ornithine. But none of these substances had effects comparable to ornithine.

3. *Discovery of reaction path.* New apparatus that he obtained at this time enabled him to determine that the nitrogen in the urea produced was comparable in quantity to the nitrogen in the ammonia consumed. He concluded that the ammonia, not the amino acids, was the source of the nitrogen. Krebs now sought to elucidate the mechanisms of the ornithine effect. It occurred to him that the (known) arginine reaction, by which arginine is converted to ornithine and urea, might be related to the ornithine effect. Concluding from the quantitative data that the ornithine could only be a catalyst, he inferred that ornithine with ammonia produces arginine, which in turn produces urea and ornithine. Later experiments indicated that citrulline was an intermediate substance between ornithine and arginine.

We must now spell out the details of Krebs' experiments and reasoning somewhat more fully, still following closely the account of Holmes. . . .

When Krebs got freedom to initiate a major research enterprise of his own, in 1931, he decided to begin experiments of the sort he had conceived. Urea synthesis was an obvious choice of a metabolic reaction that had received a great deal of attention. At the outset, he had no specific hypotheses about the reaction mechanism, but a number of more general questions: Is ammonia an obligatory intermediate; and how do rates of urea formation from various amino acids compare? These were not new questions, but Krebs thought that the tissue slice method would give him greater flexibility and more quantitative precision in seeking answers than did the methods used previously.

Krebs carried out his first experiment with alanine. The amount of urea produced in this experiment was much less than estimated according to the assumed equation of complete oxidation. Next, he compared rates of urea formation from glycine, from alanine, and from ammonium chloride, in each case with glucose present in the medium. He found very little urea formation from glycine or alanine, but substantial amounts from ammonium chloride. He also noted that the rate of formation of urea from alanine declined in the presence of glucose. Therefore, Krebs concluded that the glucose inhibited the formation of ammonia from the amino acid. He apparently accepted the received view that ammonia was an essential intermediate product, and spent about four weeks characterizing the formation of urea from ammonia: checking the quantitative relations and the necessity of aerobic conditions, and testing the effects of changes in pH. He verified that the reactions proceeded only in liver tissue. All of this work was essentially a verification of known results.

From this point on, the work was carried on with the assistance of a new medical student, Henseleit. Krebs now turned back to determining the initial source of the urea nitrogen, which he presumed to be the amino acids. Testing alanine, phenylalanine, glycine, cysteine, and cystine, he found they all produced urea at lower rates than did ammonium chloride. He also included other substances that might contribute amino groups that would be oxidized to ammonia, with the same result. Similar negative results were obtained in comparisons of ammonium chloride alone and in combination with amino acids; none of the combinations yielded urea at a higher rate than ammonium chloride alone.

During the first two weeks in November, the investigators turned to a new line of inquiry: the influence of glucose, fructose, lactate, and cetrate, all substances involved as intermediates in carbohydrate metabolism. They had no specific hypotheses, but were exploring in this direction because a difference had been found in urea production in liver slices from well-fed and starved rats.

On November 15, Henseleit was continuing these experiments, but also ran a test with the amino acid, ornithine, and with a combination of ornithine and ammonium chloride. The combination produced urea at an unexpectedly high rate, and Krebs immediately turned his attention to the ornithine effect. The laboratory logs (and Krebs' later recollections, as well) do not provide conclusive information as to why the ornithine experiment, which represented a departure from the current activity, was run at that particular time. Krebs in his recollections insisted that he took ornithine just because it was available. But Holmes speculates that he chose ornithine because the metabolic rate of ornithine was an unsolved problem. It is possible to speculate further about the reasons for the experiment, but we will leave the question unanswered here. . . .

Determination of Scope. In investigating the ornithine effect, Krebs employed "a standard biochemical strategy: if a given compound exerts some particular action, check whether derivatives of that compound have similar actions." None of the substances tested had effects similar to the ornithine effect, and Krebs became more and more convinced that the effect was quite specific to ornithine, although he had no clear hypothesis of a mechanism to account for it. This phase of the inquiry extended from the middle of November to the middle of January, 1932. . . .

Discovery of Reaction Path. On January 14, Krebs and Henseleit used, for the first time, new apparatus that permitted accurate comparison of the amounts of ammonia consumed with the amounts of urea formed. Although some of the results of the first experiments were ambiguous, it was fairly clear by January 23 that the ammonia was the precursor of all of the nitrogen in the urea.

Now some function had to be found for the ornithine, and Krebs gradually arrived at the conclusion that it served as a catalyst. While this conclusion might seem obvious to us, it was much less obvious in 1932, when the study of catalytic reactions was relatively new.

A known reaction existed, the conversion of arginine to urea and or-nithine, that could serve as the second stage of the cycle. Krebs had, in fact, studied this reaction in an experiment performed the previous October. At some point, it occurred to him that this reaction might enter into the picture. The fact that arginase is abundant in the livers of animals that excrete urea seemed significant. While Krebs was trying to conceive of a specific reaction path for the catalytic action of ornithine, he continued to direct Henseleit in experiments to elucidate further the ornithine effect, and also its interaction with arginine. During March, they also performed experiments to show spe-cifically that the ornithine effect could be obtained with very small amounts of ornithine (in relation to the amounts of urea produced), and must there-fore be catalytic. A very successful experiment of this kind was performed on April 13, in which 24.5 molecules of urea were formed for each molecule of ornithine that was present.

Gradually, Krebs inferred a specific reaction path consistent with all the known facts. On chemical grounds, it was evident that the conversion of ornithine to arginine could not proceed in a single step, and the theory was improved when Krebs found in the literature a 1930 paper reporting a sub-stance, citrulline, that had the properties of a satisfactory intermediate be-tween ornithine and arginine. Even before he obtained some citrulline, with which he could test this hypothesis, he felt sufficiently confident of his the-ory (sans the citrulline intermediate) to publish it. On April 25, five days before his paper appeared, he performed a test with citrulline, and by the middle of May, on the basis of further experiments, Krebs sent off a second paper describing the elaborated theory. The ornithine cycle as it was under-stood and depicted in 1932 is shown in [Figure 4.1]. Other researchers have since further elaborated the steps in the cycle, and the ornithine cycle as we understand today is somewhat more complex. (Kulkarni and Simon, 1988, pp. 143–147)

General Characteristics of the KEKADA Program

Intended to simulate Krebs's processes of discovery, as described by Holmes (1980), KEKADA discovery processes followed the concep-tual structure of general problem solving as developed by Simon and Lea (1974):

The overall organization of KEKADA is based on the two-space model of learning proposed by Simon & Lea (1974) shown in [Figure 4.2]. The system searches in an instance space and a role space. The possible experiments and experimental outcomes define the instance space, which is searched by per-forming experiments. The hypotheses and other higher-level descriptions, coupled with the confidences assigned to these, define the rule space. On the

Figure 4.1
The Ornithine Cycle

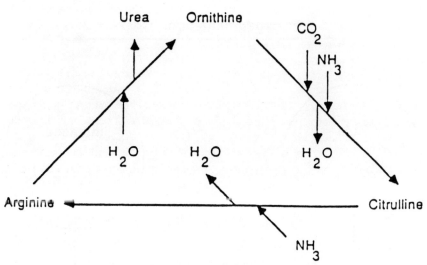

Source: D. Kulkarni and H. A. Simon, The Processes of Scientific Discovery: The Strategy of Experimentation (*Cognitive Science, 12,* 1988), p. 144. Copyright 1988 by Ablex Publishing Company. Reprinted with permission.

basis of the current state of the rule space (what hypotheses are held, with what confidences), the system chooses an experiment to carry out. The outcome of the experiment modifies the hypotheses and confidences. . . .

Operators to carry out the search in the instance space: The heuristic operators used to search the instance space fall into two categories:

1. *Experiment-proposers,* which propose experiments based on existing hypotheses.
2. *Experimenters,* which carry out experiments.

Operators to carry out the search in the rule space: The heuristic operators used to search the rule space fall in the following categories:

1. *Hypothesis or strategy proposers:* When the system has decided to focus on a particular problem, these decide which hypothesis or hypotheses to focus on or which strategy to adopt for the work on the problem.
2. *Problem-generators,* which propose new problems or subproblems on which the system can focus attention.
3. *Problem-choosers,* which choose which task the system should work on next.
4. *Expectation-setters,* which set expectations for the experiments to be carried out.
5. *Hypothesis-generators,* which generate new hypotheses about unknown mechanisms or phenomena.

Figure 4.2
Two-Space Model of Learning

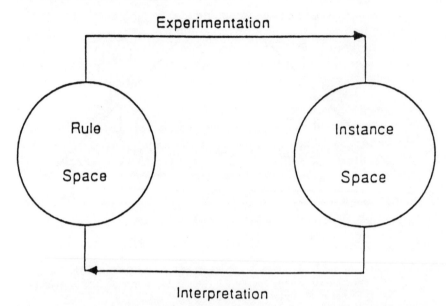

Experimentation

Rule

Space

Instance

Space

Interpretation

Source: D. Kulkarni and H. A. Simon, The Processes of Scientific Discovery: The Strategy of
Experimentation (*Cognitive Science, 12,* 1988), p. 150. Copyright 1988 by Ablex Publishing Company. Reprinted with permission.

6. *Hypothesis-modifiers,* which modify the hypotheses on the basis of new
   evidence.
7. *Confidence-modifiers,* which modify confidences about hypotheses on the
   basis of the interpretations of experiments.
   (Kulkarni and Simon, 1988, pp. 149–150)

KEKADA possesses decision-maker heuristics that determine
which of the operator heuristics are applicable at a given point in the
discovery process:

Heuristics to make choices: In KEKADA, only certain alternatives are applicable at any stage. If more than one alternative is applicable, heuristics
called *decision-makers,* are used to choose between the operators. *Decision-
makers* determine, for example, which of the various problems proposed by
problem-proposer heuristics will be worked on. (Kulkarni and Simon, 1988,
p. 150)

As KEKADA searches its problem spaces and seeks to make its
discoveries, its heuristics interact appropriately:

Interaction of Heuristics. We now can describe in more detail how the heuristics in various categories interact as the system works on a problem. If the system has not decided on which task to work (or in situations where new tasks have been added to the agenda), problem-choosers will decide which problem the system should start working on. Hypothesis-generators create hypotheses when faced with a new problem. Thus, at any given stage a certain number of hypotheses with varying confidences are present in working memory.

When working on a given task, the *hypothesis* or *strategy proposers* will choose a strategy to work on. Then the experiment-proposers will propose the experiments to be carried out. Both of these types of heuristics may need the decision-makers. Then expectation-setters set expectations and experimenters carry out experiments. The results of the experimenters are interpreted by the hypothesis modifiers and the confidence modifiers. When applicable, problem-generators may add new problems to the agenda and preempt the system to focus on a different problem. (Kulkarni and Simon, 1988, pp. 150–151)

A computer program, such as KEKADA, that attempts to simulate the discovery processes of the human scientist, must be alert to unexpected turns and results in the course of experimentation. KEKADA has mechanisms that simulate the cognitive (if not the affective) aspects of surprise that are present in the discovery process:

The ability to react to surprise, and to attempt to explain the puzzling phenomenon, plays an important role in many discoveries. KEKADA has an ability to notice a phenomenon as "surprising." Before any experiment is carried out, expectations are formed by expectation-setters and are associated with the experiment. These expectations consist of expected output substances of the reaction, and expected lower and upper bounds on the quantities or the rates of their outputs. If the results of the experiments violate these bounds, this is noted as a surprise. We give in [Figure 4.3] a slightly simplified version of the OPS5 code (See, Brownston, Farrell, Kant, & Martin, 1985) which implements the PG1 heuristics: if the outcome of an experiment violates the expectations for it, then make the study of this puzzling phenomenon a task and add it to the agenda. The bold lines beginning with a semicolon (;) are comments about the OPS5 code. (Kulkarni and Simon, 1988, p. 151)

KEKADA must not only be able to recognize surprises and puzzling events occurring in the experimental process, but it must also be able to advance hypotheses that guide the continuation of exploration:

Figure 4.3
OPS5 Code for the Surprise-Detector Heuristic

```
;Name of the rule
(p note-surprise

  ;LEFT HAND SIDE (Condition of the rule)
  ;if this rule is of type problem-generator
  (context ^name problem-generator)
  ;if given experiment with inputs <i1>,<i2>,and<i3>is found to
  ; to have output <o> and the rate-of-output <r-o>
  (experiment ^status just-done ^input1<i1> ^input2<i2> ^input3<i3>
          ^expected-output <e-o>
          ^expected-lower-bound <lb> ^expected-upper bound <ub>
          ^output <o> ^rate-of-output <r-o>)
  ;and if expectations set with the experiment are: output <e-o>
  ; upper-bound on the output-rate <ub>, and
  ; lower-bound on the output-rate <lb>
  ; and if the results of the experiment violate these expectations
  -(experiment ^status just-done ^input1<i1> ^input2<i2> ^input3<i3>
          ^expected-output <e-o>
          ^expected-lower-bound <lb> ^expected-upper-bound <ub>
          ^output <e-o> ^rate-of-output { >=<lb> <=<ub>})

  ;THEN
  ->

  ;RIGHT HAND SIDE (Action taken if the condition is met)
  ;Note this as a surprise and add to the agenda, with associated
  ;information on actual and expected outputs.
  (bind<newid>)
  (make agenda ^task-name<newid>)
  (make surprise ^name<newid> ^input1<i1> ^input2<i2> ^input3<i3>
          ^expected-output <e-o>
          ^expected-lower-bound <lb> ^expected-upper-bound <ub>
          ^output <o> ^rate-of-output <r-o>)
```

Source: D. Kulkarni and H. A. Simon, The Processes of Scientific Discovery: The Strategy of Experimentation (*Cognitive Science, 12,* 1988), p. 153. Copyright 1988 by Ablex Publishing Company. Reprinted with permission.

Hypothesis-generators

[HG1] If a surprising outcome occurs involving A as one of the reactants, then hypothesize that there is a class of substances containing A (or its derivatives) that will produce the same outcome.

[HG2] If there is a surprisingly low output of substance A under some experimental conditions but not others, and if it is possible that another substance S is present in the latter conditions but not the former, hypothesize that the absence of S is causing the low output.

[HG3] If a reaction has subprocesses and the outcome of the reaction is surprising, hypothesize that the surprising result depends on one of the subprocesses (divide and conquer strategy).

[HG4] If a reaction produces some output, create hypotheses asserting which reactant donates which group to the output substance and that a reactant may be a catalyst.

[HG5] If a one-step stereochemical transformation from inputs to outputs of a reaction is not possible, then create the hypothesis that an intermediate exists. Otherwise create a hypothesis that there is a one-step stereochemical reaction.

[HG6] If the goal is to study a puzzling phenomenon and if the given reaction and the surprising phenomenon contain two common substances, then create a hypothesis that they may be related.

[HG7] If the output from A and from B is different from the sum of the outputs from A and B, then create hypothesis that there is mixed action from A and B otherwise create the hypothesis that the effect is additive.

[HG8] Properties of a class are true for a member. (Kulkarni and Simon, 1988, pp. 156–157)

Krebs began his work with a certain technical knowledge. During the course of his work, he acquired additional knowledge from scientific journals and from professional colleagues. All this knowledge influenced the choice and course of his experimentation. In order to simulate the onset and course of Krebs's experiments and discoveries, KEKADA was provided with the same knowledge:

Background Knowledge. The background knowledge takes two forms. Some of it is contained in domain-specific heuristics embedded in KEKADA, that are described in previous subsections. Other knowledge is created by using "make" statements before KEKADA is run. "Make" statements create initial working memory elements of various kinds. These working memory elements constitute the system's initial knowledge. Prior knowledge falls in 3 categories: knowledge about substances, knowledge about processes, and knowledge about previous experiments.

1. Knowledge about substances including the amino acids, glucose, and so forth, includes their chemical formulae, cost, availability and the class to which they belong. KEKADA also knows the typical low, medium and high quantity of a substance to be used in the experiments. Besides KEKADA knows the partial order relation stating which of two substances is more similar to a given substance.

2. KEKADA also has knowledge about chemical reactions. This includes the

inputs, the outputs, the class to which the reaction belongs and some supplementary facts. When the exact place or condition under which the process takes place is not known, supplementary facts may give various possible
places or conditions where the process might be taking place. Also associated with each supplementary fact is the confidence that the process does
take place at this place. The knowledge also includes various possibilities
previously considered likely regarding where the process takes place.

3. Before Krebs undertook the research program that led to the ornithine
   cycle discovery, he had read about the experiments others had carried out
   on urea synthesis. It is assumed that his initial expectations about the outcomes were set either by the previous experiments or by some previously
   known theory. Therefore, the summary of these previous experiments is
   made available to KEKADA. KEKADA uses this knowledge only to set the
   expectations for the initial experiments.

Acquiring Knowledge Through Literature and from Colleagues. Apart from
the results of his own experiments, Krebs' research was also influenced by
such factors as the availability of a new instrument and the research results
published by other scientists. Correspondingly, OPS5 allows the creation of
new working memory elements at intermediate stages in the progress of KE-
KADA to allow such factors to enter. (Kulkarni and Simon, 1988, pp.
159–160)

KEKADA's Simulation of Krebs's Discoveries

In this section, an extended example of KEKADA's discovery processes and comparison with Krebs's discovery processes are presented.
The example of KEKADA's discovery processes takes the form of a
log of its performance:

Simulation of the Discovery of the Ornithine Cycle

We present here the log of a particular run of KEKADA described in terms
of the numbered heuristics we have described. An asterisk (*) denotes repeated application of a set of heuristics. Seq*i* names the sequence of firings
of heuristics that is enclosed in the following pair of dashed lines. [Explana-
tion of the abbreviations for heuristics is given in Table 4.3]

Heuristics	*Results*
PC0	Considers various alternative tasks on the agenda. Considers as possible candidates urea synthesis and synthesis of some fats, proteins, and fatty acid degradation, etc.
PC1–7*	Chooses urea synthesis from among the various alternatives and creates a goal to study urea synthesis using the tissue slice method.
HSC1	Considers alternative hypotheses on urea synthesis,

Table 4.3
General Heuristics in KEKADA

CATEGORY OF HEURISTICS	DOMAIN-INDEPENDENT	NO	DOMAIN-SPECIFIC	NO
PROBLEM CHOOSERS	PCO-8	9		
PROBLEM GENERATORS	PG1	1		
DECISION-MAKERS	DM1-4	4	DM5-10	6
EXPERIMENT-PROPOSERS	EP1,EP6,EP7	3	EP2-5,EP8	5
EXPECTATION-SETTERS	ES1-4	4		
HYPOTHESIS-GENERATORS	HG1,3,8	3	HG2,4,5,6,7	5
HYPOTHESIS-MODIFIERS	HM4-5	2	HM1-3,B1-11,HM6	15
CONFIDENCE-MODIFIERS	CF3,CF4,CF5	3	CF1,2	2
HYPOTHESIS/STRATEGY CHOOSERS	HSC1,HSC2	2		
BACKGROUND KNOWLEDGE			DOMAIN-SPECIFIC	
TOTAL		31		33

Source: D. Kulkarni and H. A. Simon, The Processes of Scientific Discovery: The Strategy of Experimentation (*Cognitive Science, 12,* 1988), p. 172. Copyright 1988 by Ablex Publishing Company. Reprinted with permission.

	viz., amino acids may produce urea, pyrimidines may do so, cynates may be precursors to urea, etc.
DM4*	Considers it likely that amino acids may produce urea.
EP1	Considers various amino acids as alternatives.
DM5-8*	Chooses alanine.
HG8	Assigns to alanine the properties of the class, amino acid.
EP2-3	Decides for an experiment on alanine and on ammonia. Decides for an experiment on both combined together.
ES1-3*	Sets expectations for these experiments.
E1, ES4, CF1-2*	Asks user for the results of experiments, modifies confidences.
PG1, PC8	Notes the result of the experiment on alanine as surprising, and makes it focus of attention, creates the following hypotheses:

HG5, B1–11*	Studies alanine to urea reaction, *decides that intermediate exists.*
HG2	*Some essential substance is missing from the tissue slice preparation.*
HG3	*The reason for surprise may be one of the subreactions.*
HG1*	*The phenomenon may be common to some or all elements of a class.*
[seq0]	

[Begin seq0]	
HSC1	Evaluates the alternatives.
DM4,9*	Decides to consider the hypothesis that an absence of a substance may be causing the surprise.
EP6	Guesses the substances which may be present — various substances involved in carbohydrate mechanism.
DM5*	Chooses glucose.
ES3	Sets expectations for the experiment.
E1, ES4	Asks user for output for an experiment on alanine and glucose.
CF3	Modifies failed-effort slot in hypothesis.
[End seq0]	

[Repeats seq0 for various substances.]	
HM4	Makes inactive the existential hypothesis that there may be a substance missing.
HSC1	Evaluates the alternatives.
DM4, 9*	Decides to consider the hypothesis that the cause of the process may be in one of the subprocesses.
HSC2, DM1	Decides to study the subprocess of urea synthesis from ammonia.
EP7, ES1, E1, ES4, CF4–5*	Carries out experiments on urea formation on ammonia under various conditions of pH, aerobicity and in various organs, study quantitative relations.
[seq1]	

[Begin seq1]	
HSC1	Evaluates the alternatives.
DM4*	Decides to consider the third hypothesis: that surprise may be limited to a class.
EP1	Decides to list possible amino acids for consideration.
DM5-8*	Chooses cysteine.
HG8	Assigns properties of the class to cysteine.

EP2-3	Decides for an experiment on cysteine and on ammonia. Decides for an experiment on both combined together.
ES1-3, E1, ES4, CF1.2*	Sets expectations for these experiments. Asks user for the results of the experiment. Modifies the confidences in hypotheses.
[End seq1]	

[Repeats seq1 on other amino acids, last one being ornithine.]

PG1, PC8	Notices the ornithine effect and makes it the focus of attention. Creates following hypothesis.
HG7	New clue is created for *mixed action of both the inputs.*
HG4*	*Hypotheses about who donates what to the reaction.*
HG5, B1-11*	*Intermediate exists.*
HG4	*Possibility that ornithine or ammonia is catalyst.*
HG1*	*Possibility that the phenomenon may be common to a class of substances.*
HG6*	*Possibility of relation to similar reactions.*
[seq2]	

[Begin seq2]	
HSC1	Evaluates the alternatives.
DM4-9*	Decides to study the scope of the phenomenon. Considers that the phenomenon may be common to amino acids.
EP1	Considers various amino acids.
DM5-8*	Decides on an amino acid as the choice.
HG8	Assigns properties of the class to that amino acid.
EP2-3	Decides for an experiment on the amino acid leucine and on ammonia, separately and combined.
ES1-3, E1, ES4, CF-3*	Sets expectations for these experiments. Asks user for the results of experiments. Changes the implied . . . failure in hypotheses about how urea is formed reduce the failed-effort slot in the hypothesis asserting that the phenomenon may be common to a class.
[End seq2]	

[Repeats [seq2] for various amino-acids]

| HM4 | Removes the description that some amino acids might produce urea. |
| [seq3] | |

[Begin seq3]

HSC1	Evaluates the alternatives.
DM4-9*	Decides to study the hypothesis that the scope to the surprise may be common to some or all amines.
EP1	Considers various amines.
DM5-8*	Decides on putrescine. Decides for an experiment on putrescine and ammonia.
HG8	Assigns the properties of its class to putrescine.
ES3, E1,	
ES4, CF3	Sets expectations for these experiments. Asks user for the results of experiments. Reduces the failed-effort slot in the hypothesis asserting that the phenomenon may be common to a class.

[End seq3]

[Repeats [seq3] for various amines.]

HM4	Removes description that some amines might produce urea.

[Repeats [seq3] for various carboxylic acids.]

HM4	Removes description that some carboxylic acids might produce urea.
HSC1	Evaluates the various alternatives.
DM10	User decides to study the hypothesis that source of NH_2 group in urea is ammonia.
EP4, ES1, E1	Carries out the experiment after setting expectations.
HM6	Concludes that the source of amino group is NH_3.
HSC1	Evaluates the various alternatives.
DM10	User chooses to study the related reaction: arginine reaction.
EP8, DM10	Two possible hypotheses are created: *arginine may be intermediate, or there may be a class of substances exhibiting reaction similar to arginine reaction.* Considers the second hypothesis.
EP1	Considers substances in guanidino class.
DM5*	Chooses guanidine as substance for reaction.
EP1	Decides for the reaction on guanidine and ammonia.
HG8	Assigns properties of the class to guanidine.
ES3,E1,	
ES4,CF3	Carries out the experiment. Reduces the confidence in the existential hypothesis.
HSC1–DM10	Chooses the possibility that ornithine is catalyst.
EP5	Decides for an experiment to verify catalysis.
E1	Carries out experiments to check catalysis.
HM1	Concludes that ornithine acts as a catalyst.
B1-11*	Balances the catalysis reaction.
HG5	*Creates hypothesis that there exists intermediate in the reaction.*

HM2,B1–11*	*Creates candidates for intermediate.* Balances the re-actions. Counts the number of inputs. Evaluates the intermediates. Chooses arginine.
HG5	*Creates a hypothesis that there exists intermediate in the reaction.*

(User, when asked to carry out a survey, creates elements corresponding to citrulline and other substances.)

HM2,B–11*	*Considers candidate substances* which are structurally intermediate between the inputs and the outputs of the ornithine to arginine reaction. Balances the reactions. Counts the number of inputs. Evaluates the plausibility of the candidate substances and chooses citrulline from them.

(Kulkarni and Simon, 1988, pp. 160–164)

The log of KEKADA's behavior depicts in detail pathways to discovery that parallel Holmes's (1980) description of Krebs's sequences of discovery steps (discussed earlier). The way in which KEKADA's behavior paralleled that of Krebs is clearly discernible in Figure 4.4, which groups the details of the log into larger units that delineate the course of the research and the stages of the ornithine discovery.

Kulkarni and Simon (1988) concluded that not only does KE-KADA succeed in its simulation, but that it also "constitutes a theory of Krebs' style of experimentation" (p. 143):

In the introduction, we argued that Holmes' reconstruction of Krebs' discovery of ornithine cycle is reliable data on which to build a theory of discovery. Now, if we compare the course of work of Krebs with that of KEKADA, we find that there are only minor differences, which can be explained by focus of attention shifts and small differences in the initial knowledge with which KEKADA and Krebs started. Apart from these differences, KEKADA follows the same strategy of experimentation as Krebs and its motivations for carrying out various experiments are the same as the motivations of Krebs whenever these are indicated by evidence in the diaries and retrospective interviews. As KEKADA accounts for the data on Krebs' research, it constitutes a theory of Krebs' style of experimentation. Next, we must ask how general this theory is. (Kulkarni and Simon, 1988, p. 171)

KEKADA as a General Simulator of the Scientific Discovery Process

From the point of view of Kulkarni and Simon (1988), the processes of scientific discovery, whether those of Krebs or any other sci-

Figure 4.4
Progress of KEKADA in the Discovery

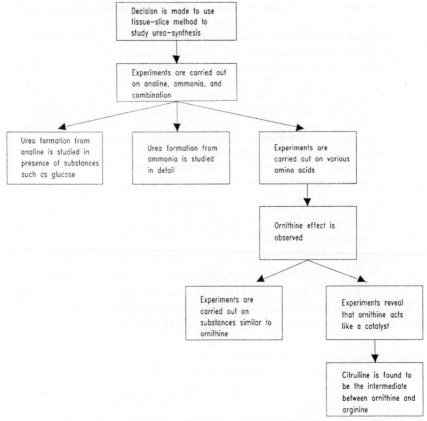

Source: D. Kulkarni and H. A. Simon, The Processes of Scientific Discovery: The Strategy of
Experimentation (*Cognitive Science, 12,* 1988), p. 165. Copyright 1988 by Ablex Publishing Company. Reprinted with permission.

entist, can be represented as a goal-directed series of problem-solving
steps that are guided by domain-directed knowledge and by heuristic
operators that are both domain-specific and domain-general. The
KEKADA system simulates this theory of the nature of the scientific
discovery process.

(1) KEKADA contains many general heuristics that are applicable in a large
    number of situations. [Table 4.3] shows that KEKADA has 31 domain-
    independent and 33 domain-specific heuristics. The domain-independent
    heuristics are some that scientists in various disciplines continue to use in
    making discoveries. Of domain-specific heuristics, DM5 to DM10 are ac-

tually applications to chemistry of more general domain-independent heuristics. Of the other domain-specific heuristics, for all except B*, DM9 and EP3 we have historical evidence (Baldwin, 1947; Fruton, 1972; Holmes, 1986, personal communication; Luck, 1932) that they were in common use in the study of metabolic reactions in biochemistry in the early 20th century, before 1931 and for some years later. Thus, they constituted accepted domain-specific strategies which a newcomer like Krebs was likely to know after a brief introduction to the field. The B* heuristics are also quite general in their applicability, for they can be used to balance not only the reactions in this discovery, but many other reactions as well.

(2) As is shown in the log [in the previous section], most of KEKADA's heuristics are used a number of times in the particular scenario given. EP8, HG2, HG7, and HM1 are the only domain-specific heuristics that are fired only once, but their potential utility in other research situations is clear.

(3) Some of KEKADA's heuristics were also used in different forms by AM, a mathematical discovery system, in the course of a wide variety of discoveries (Davis & Lenat, 1980).

(4) Thanks to Holmes (1986, personal communication), we now have data on a second major discovery of Hans Krebs, that of glutamine synthesis. A hand simulation indicates that, the path Krebs followed there is wholly consistent with the current theory. We will report in more detail on the KEKADA simulation of the research on glutamine synthesis in another study.

These considerations show that although KEKADA was handcrafted to fit our knowledge of the procedures Krebs used in his discovery of the urea cycle, the structure and the heuristics it embodies constitute a model of wider applicability. (Kulkarni and Simon, 1988, pp. 171, 173)

Commentary

At the beginning of this section, it was stated that the general logic of computational theories of scientific discovery includes a set of general assumptions. The research of Kulkarni and Simon (1988) on the KEKADA system will be used to examine these assumptions and, to that extent, to evaluate the logic of computational theories of scientific discovery.

The assumption that the processes of creativity in scientific discovery has a knowable character can be supported once it is granted that some degree of confidence can be placed in Holmes's (1980) account, and that Krebs's logs and recollections of the onset, course, and outcome of his experimentation possess an acceptable level of completeness and reliability. The assumption that the creative processes of scientific discovery are definable can be supported given KEKADA's definitional heuristics which include the capacity for planning and executing experiments, the recognition of surprising experimental results, and the consequent revision of hypotheses and continuation of the control strategies of systematic experimentation.

The assumption that scientific discovery processes represent subsets of general problem-solving strategies is supported by the two-space (an instant space and a rule space) model of problem solving (Simon and Lea, 1974) which provided the general superstructure for the development of the control logic in the KEKADA system. KEKADA's success in replicating Hans Krebs's scientific discoveries would appear to support the understanding of scientific discovery as a special case of the two-space problem-solving theory.

The assumption that scientific discovery processes can be modelled by the standard heuristics of computational problem-solving systems is supported by the use in KEKADA of the familiar artificial intelligence methodology of the production system. In addition, KEKADA's possession of a large set of general heuristics, potentially applicable to scientific discovery problems beyond those of Krebs, lends credence to the assumption that a computational system such as KEKADA can model general aspects of the process of scientific discovery.

The assumption that a computational system such as KEKADA can make original and independent discoveries is difficult to evaluate. To KEKADA, as to Krebs, the discoveries were new. To the scientific world, KEKADA's discoveries were replications and rediscoveries. The metabolic processes of the ornithine cycle were disclosed by Krebs, and that disclosure was repeated by KEKADA. The developers (Kulkarni and Simon, 1988) cannot claim for KEKADA the status of making an original contribution to contemporary knowledge in the field of biochemistry.

The general logic of the computational theory of scientific discovery processes should be contrasted with theories of human scientific discovery that characterize or require the existence of intrinsic motivation. Theories of the nature of human creativity (Sternberg, 1988) are in general agreement that the conditions for creativity require inherent interest in the subject and love for the creative task:

Guiding our investigations is what we have termed the *intrinsic motivation principle of creativity:*

People will be most creative when they feel motivated primarily by the interest, enjoyment, satisfaction, and challenge of the work itself — not by external pressures.

In essence, we are saying that the love people feel for their work has a great deal to do with the creativity of their performances. This proposition is clearly supported by accounts of the phenomenology of creativity. Most reports from and about creative individuals are filled with notions of an intense involvement in and unrivaled love for their work. Thomas Mann, for example, described in one of his letters his passion for writing (John-Steiner, 1985), and physicists who were close to Albert Einstein saw in him a similar kind of intensity. In the words of the Nobel Prize–winning inventor Dennis Gabor, "no one has ever enjoyed science as much as Einstein" (John-Steiner, 1985, p. 67)
(Hennessey and Amabile, 1988, p. 11)

Since I reached the conclusion that the essence of the creative person is being in love with what one is doing, I have had a growing awareness that this characteristic makes possible all the other personality characteristics of the creative person: courage, independence of thought and judgement, honesty, perseverance, curiosity, willingness to take risks, and the like. For example, Roger Tory Peterson (Beebe, 1986) at a very young age was in love with nature, especially birds. He was a social outcast in his youth because of this. . . . This has been a common experience of many of our most eminent inventors, scientists, artists, musicians, writers, and so on. To maintain an intense love for something and survive these kinds of pressures, one has to develop courage, independence, perseverance, and the like. (Torrance, 1988, p. 68)

I want to know how God created this world. I am not interested in this or that phenomenon, in the spectrum of this or that element. I want to know His thoughts, the rest are details. (Albert Einstein, quoted in Ferris, 1988, p. 177)

Once the validity of this mode of thought has been recognized, the final results appear almost simple; any intelligent undergraduate can understand them without much trouble. But the years of searching in the dark for a truth that one feels, but cannot express; the intense desire and the alternations of confidence and misgiving, until one breaks through to charity and understanding, are only known to him who has himself experienced them. (Albert Einstein, quoted in Ferris, 1988, p. 177)

Clearly, computational theories of discovery do not require that the computational system possess intrinsic motivation as a necessary condition for creativity. The heuristic mechanisms of computational systems are sufficient.

Finally, it is not clear that the use of a scientist's laboratory logs and recollections is adequate for areas of science that, unlike the rather applied bench experimentation of Krebs, depend on complex reflection, deep theory, and thought experimentation, as exemplified in the creative processes of Albert Einstein. It remains to be seen whether the intellectual levels of advanced theoretical science can be encompassed by computational theories of scientific discovery.

There is no inductive method which could lead to the fundamental concepts of physics. . . .[I]n error are those theorists who believe that theory comes inductively from experience. (Albert Einstein, 1933, p. 177)

HUMAN COGNITION AND A MODEL OF SCIENTIFIC DISCOVERY PROCESSES

The General Logic of Scientific Discovery Processes

The nature of the human cognitive processes that lead to scientific discoveries has been a matter of great interest to scientists themselves, as well as to philosophers and historians of science, to theoretical and experimental psychologists, and, most recently, to cognitive scientists who develop computational models of scientific discovery. Many scientists have written accounts of their intellectual struggles and creative insights.

In the seventeenth century, Johannes Kepler wrote *De Motibus Stellae Martis,* in which he recounted his years of intellectual struggle to reconcile conflicts between geocentrism and heliocentrism, and between the physical data of the orbit of Mars and the mathematical representation of the orbit as circular or elliptical (Kepler, 1937). In the nineteenth century, Charles Darwin wrote *The Origin of Species* ([1872] 1936), in which he recorded his years of intellectual effort to reconcile conflicts between his developing theory of natural selection and traditional religious beliefs.

There is a grandeur in this view of life, with its several powers, having been originally breathed by the Creator into a few forms or into one; and that, whilst this planet has gone cycling on according to the fixed law of gravity, from so simple a beginning endless forms most beautiful and most wonderful have been, and are being evolved. (Darwin, [1872], 1936, p. 374)

For both Kepler and Darwin, scientific discovery occurred over a long period of time, punctuated by many baffling dilemmas and resolved by many minor and major insights rather than by a singularly dramatic flash of all-illuminating creative insight (Gruber and Davis, 1988). Nonetheless, in the twentieth century, H. Poincare reported just such a sudden insight into a mathematics problem that had long frustrated him:

Just at this time, I left Caen, where I was then living, to go on a geological excursion under the auspices of the school of mines. The changes of travel made me forget my mathematical work. Having reached Coutances, we entered an omnibus to go some place or another. At the moment when I put my foot on the step the idea came to me, without anything in my former thoughts seeming to have paved the way for it, that the transformations I had used to define the Fuschisan functions were identical with those on non-Euclidean geometry. I did not verify the idea; I should not have had time, as, upon taking my seat in the omnibus, I went on with a conversation already commenced, but I felt a perfect certainty. On my return to Caen, for conscience' sake I verified the result at my leisure. (Poincare, 1913, pp. 287 288)

Similarly, James Watson, after years of laboratory experimentation and construction, and after the rejection of numerous molecular genetic models, reported his lucid and sudden discovery that the double helix was the correct model.

Suddenly I became aware that an adenine–thymine pair held together by two hydrogen bonds was identical in shape to a guanine–cytosine pair held together by at least two hydrogen bonds. *All the hydrogen bonds seemed to form naturally; no fudging was required to make the two types of base pairs identical in shape. . . .* I suspected that we now had the answer to the riddle of why the number of purine residues exactly equaled the number of pyrimidine residues. Two irregular sequences of bases could be regularly packed in the center of a helix if a purine always hydrogen-bonded to a pyrimidine. Furthermore, the hydrogen-bonding requirement meant that adenine would always pair with thymine, while guanine could pair only with cytosine. *Chargaff's roles then suddenly stood out as a consequence of a double-helical structure for DNA.* Even more exciting, this type of double helix suggested a replication scheme much more satisfactory than my briefly considered like-with-like pairing. Always pairing adenine with thymine and guanine with cytosine meant that the base sequences of the two intertwined chains were complementary to each other. Given the base sequence of one chain, that of its partner was automatically determined. *Conceptually, it was thus very easy to visualize how a single chain could be the template for the synthesis of a chain with the complementary sequence.* (Watson, 1968, pp. 194–196, italics added)

In the general logic of the scientific discovery process, the differential centrality of a single and sudden insight (Poincare and Watson) or of many and gradual insights (Kepler and Darwin) may be related to the scope or breadth of the scientific discovery: (a) The search for a general theory of biological forms and development or the search for a general theory of the solar system and its laws of planetary revolution, versus (b) the search for the proof of a specific mathematical theorem or the search for a specific geometrical model of genetic information.

Cognitive scientists such as Herbert Simon have attempted to demonstrate that some scientific discoveries are simply the discernment of a sequence of periodicity of a set of instances, such as the discovery by Dmitri Mendeleev that instances of chemical elements can be arranged as a sequence of increasing molecular weights. Simon (1977) characterized Mendeleev's discovery process as the induction of a rule that fits the instances or data.

Consider, for example, the Periodic Law of Mendeleev. Discovering this law involves arranging the elements by the successor relation with respect to atomic weight, and then noting the periodic repetition of certain chemical properties (e.g., valence) in this list. . . .

Mendeleev's Periodic Table does not involve a notion of pattern more complex than that required to handle patterned letter sequences. To be sure, Mendeleev had to conjecture that atomic weight was the attribute according to which the elements should be ordered. But it should be observed that he made his discovery just a few years after the notion of atomic weight had been clarified, its central importance had been accepted, and the atomic weights of most of the known elements had been determined. The space of possible (or plausible) patterns in which Mendeleev was searching was perhaps of rather modest size. And, indeed, at least a half dozen of Mendeleev's contemporaries had noticed the pattern independently of him, although they had not exploited it as systematically or vigorously as he did.

Before we accept the hypothesis, therefore, that "revolutionary science" is not subject to laws of effective search we would do well to await n = more microscopic studies than have generally been made to date of the histories of revolutionary discoveries. The case of Mendeleev may prove to be not at all exceptional. At present, one can argue this only as a possibility. But as long as it is a possibility, we must receive with skepticism arguments that would seek to prove the "impossibility" of the logic of scientific discovery—even revolutionary discovery. (Simon, 1977, pp. 333–335)

More formally, according to Simon and Lea (1974), the general logic of the scientific discovery process can be construed as search in two problem spaces; an instance space of data or experiments, and a rule space of hypotheses or theories. Kulkarni and Simon (1988), using this logic of scientific discovery, developed the KEKADA system, which replicated (or rediscovered) Hans Krebs's discovery of the ornithine cycle (see section on artificial intelligence and the processes of scientific discovery in this chapter). Similarly, the BACON.3 system (Langley, 1981) rediscovered Kepler's laws of the solar system, and the AM system (Lenat, 1977) rediscovered the concept of prime numbers (see section on artificial intelligence and the processes of scientific discovery in this chapter).

Laboratory experiments that simulate aspects of the scientific discovery process constitute another approach to studying the cognition of scientific discovery. Such studies provide a microcosm for discerning the processes of hypothesis formation, experimental design, and interpretative conclusion. Such laboratory studies may also lead to a useful model of the nature and logic of the scientific discovery process. In this section, a representative example of this type of laboratory study will be discussed (Klahr and Dunbar, 1988).

The Discovery Process and Its Simulation

D. Klahr and K. Dunbar (1988) conceptualized the discovery process as the cyclical operation of three variables: knowledge, hypothesis, and experimentation. The goal is the discovery of new knowledge. In the cycle, initial knowledge leads to a search in a hypothesis space and in an experiment space. Within the hypothesis space, a hypothesis is selected and a prediction is made. Within the experiment space, an experiment is designed to test the prediction. The disconfirmation or confirmation of the prediction provides knowledge which the scientist evaluates. The evaluation leads to a decision that the goal has been attained or that the cycle of operations should be repeated. In order to test their conceptualization of the scientific discovery process, Klahr and Dunbar designed a laboratory simulation of the discovery process that would provide a controlled investigation of the fine details of the process. From the findings of their experimental research, they intended to develop a formal model of the scientific discovery process.

The simulation of the scientific discovery process was the discovery, by undergraduate university students, of the nature of a specific mechanism in BigTrak, a programmable robot:

BigTrak

The device we use is a computer-controlled robot tank (called "BigTrak") that is programmed using a LOGO-like language. It is a six-wheeled, battery-powered vehicle, approximately 30 cm long, 20 cm wide, and 15 cm high. Interaction takes place via a keypad on the top of the device, which is illustrated in [Figure 4.5]. In order to get BigTrak to behave, the user clears the memory with the *CLR* key and then enters a series of up to 16 instructions, each consisting of a function key (the command) and a 1- or 2-digit number (the argument), terminated by the *GO* key. BigTrak then executes the program by moving around on the floor.

The effect of the argument depends on which command it follows. For forward (↑) and backward (↓) motion, each unit corresponds to approximately one foot. For left (←) and right (→) turns, the unit is a 6° rotation (corresponding to one minute on a clock face. Thus, a 90° turn is 15 "minutes.") The *HOLD* unit is a delay (or pause) of 0.1 second, and the *FIRE* unit is one auditory event: the firing of the cannon (indicated by appropriate sound and light effects). The other keys shown in [Figure 4.5] are *CLS, CK,* and *RPT. CLS* Clears the Last Step (i.e., the most recently entered instruction) by executing it in isolation. Using *CK* does not effect the contents of memory. We will describe *RPT* later. The *GO, CLR, CLS,* and *CK* commands do not take an argument. To illustrate, one might press the following series of keys:

CLR ↑ 5 ← 7 ↓ 3 → 15 HOLD 50 FIRE 2 ↓ 8 GO

and BigTrak would do the following: move forward five feet, rotate counterclockwise 42°, move forward 3 feet, rotate clockwise 90°, pause for 5 seconds, fire twice, and back up 8 feet.

Figure 4.5
The Keypad from the BigTrak Robot

Source: D. Klahr and K. Dunbar, Dual Space Search during Scientific Reasoning (*Cognitive Science, 12,* 1988), p. 8. Copyright 1988 by Ablex Publishing Company. Reprinted with permission.

Certain combinations of keystrokes (e.g., a third numerical digit or two motion commands without an intervening numerical argument) are not permitted by the syntax of the programming language. With each syntactically legal keystroke, BigTrak emits an immediate, confirmatory beep. Syntactically illegal keystrokes elicit no response, and they are not entered into program memory. (Klahr and Dunbar, 1988, pp. 8-9)

The First Experimental Study of the Discovery Process

The experimental study had two phases: a training phase and a discovery phase. The procedure for the training phase was as follows:

First, we established a common knowledge base about the device for all subjects, *prior to the discovery phase.* . . . We instructed subjects about how to use all function keys and special keys, except for *RPT.* Subjects learned about the syntax and semantics of the keys and about how to combine commands into a program to accomplish some goal. All subjects were trained to criterion on the keys described earlier and given a fixed set of tasks to accomplish. (Klahr and Dunbar, 1988, p. 10)

The experimental procedure for the discovery phase was as follows:

Subjects were told that there is a "repeat" key, that it takes a numerical parameter, and that there can be only one *RPT* in a program. *Then, they were asked to discover how* RPT *works by proposing hypotheses and evaluating them.* (We suggest that before going further, the reader do the following: formulate an initial hypothesis about how *RPT* works, and then construct a BigTrak program to evaluate the hypothesis. This will provide a subjective impression of the task facing the subject.) (Klahr and Dunbar, 1988, p. 10, italics added)

The subjects' verbalized statements, made in the process of discovering the nature of the *RPT* key, were encoded as follows:

Explicit statements about how the subject thought the *RPT* key might work were coded as hypotheses. Statements of what might happen once the *GO* had been pressed were coded as predictions. Comments about the behavior of the device once the program had been executed were coded as observations. (Klahr and Dunbar, 1988, p. 12)

An example of the encoding procedure is the following:

To illustrate, we will give an example of the encoding of an entire protocol. (The listing, shown in [Table 4.4] is one of our shortest, because it was gen-

Table 4.4

Example of a Complete Protocol (CLR and GO commands have been deleted)

002   *EXP: SO HOW DO YOU THINK IT MIGHT WORK?*
003   *Uh... it would repeat all of the steps before it, however many times*
004   *I told it to repeat it.*
005   *EXP: WELL... SO START WORKING ON IT NOW THEN.*
006   *Ok.*
007   *EXP: AND TELL ME EVERYTHING THATS GOING ON IN YOUR MIND.*
008   *Ok.*
009   *EXP: NOW PRESS CLEAR.*
010   *Ok, um... I'm gonna to make it go*
011   *forward two, and then I'm gonna make it repeat that twice.*

012 *00:30 | 2 RPT 2*

                                                                        | 4

013   *Maybe not, uh...... repeat once*

014 *02:00 | 1 - 15 | 1 HOLD 2 RPT 1*

                                  | 1 - 15 | 1 HOLD 4

015   *Hmm.. guess that was it.*
016   *EXP: SO WHAT ARE YOU THINKING?*
017   *Um.. actually I have no idea now.*
018   *I'm trying to figure out what it is.*
019   *Um.. maybe it repeats the last step.*
020   *Ok, I'm gonna try that. ..... repeat once.*

021 *03:30 | 2 - 30 RPT 1*

                                        | 2 - 60

022   *All right, that backs up my theory.*
023   *Let me see if I can somehow make sure that that's what it does*
024   *is repeats the last step however many times that I tell it to,*
025   *so I'm gonna ... repeat it four times ...*

026 *04:00 | 2 - 30 RPT 4*

                                  | 2 - 30 | 2 - 30

027
028   *That was strange, hmm... um... let me see that again.*

029 *04:30 | 2 - 30 RPT 4*

                                  | 2 - 30 | 2 - 30

030   *Ok, maybe it means repeat the last number...*
031   *however many steps before it that I put in,*
032   *that'll be the number after the repeat. For instance,*
033   *if I put repeat two, it'll repeat the last two steps,*
034   *if I put repeat five, it'll repeat the last five steps,*
035   *and if there's too many...*

036   *if the five is more than the number of steps in the progam,*
037   *it'll just end it at whatever number of steps in the program,*
038   *so . . . repeat one, no, repeat two.*
039
040 06:00 | 2 - 15 | 2 FIRE 3 RPT 2

                                   | 2 - 15 | 2 FIRE 3 | 2 FIRE 3

041   *All right, I think I might have gotten it.*
042

043 06:30 | 2 - 15 | 2 FIRE 3 RPT 3

                                   | 2 - 15 | 2 FIRE 3 - 15 | 2 FIRE 3

044   *Ok, I think I've gotten it. I'm gonna make it repeat four times.*
045   *. . . wanna repeat four...*

046 07:30 | 2 - 15 | 2 FIRE 3 RPT 4

                              | 2 - 15 | 2 FIRE 3 | 2 - 15 | 2 FIRE 3

047   *Ok, now I'm trying to figure out which order the repeat step goes.*
048   *If it does the first part of the program or if it does...if it starts*
049   *from the last part of the program, where repeat...*
050   *if I say repeat one, does it repeat the first step in the program,*
051   *or does it repeat the last step I pressed in? Um... repeat that*
052   *step...*
053
054 09:00 | 2 - 15 | 2 FIRE 3 RPT 1

                                     | 2 - 15 | 2 FIRE 6

055
056   *It goes from the last step,*
057   *and I don't understand why it doesn't go backwards.*
058   *Maybe it counts back two steps.*
059   *If I put repeat two, it would count back two steps,*
060   *starting from there and go until the last step. Alright,*
061   *...um... the last two steps were forward two and fire three,*
062   *so let me try and repeat that again.*

063 10:00 | 2 - 15 | 2 FIRE 3 RPT 2

                              | 2 - 15 | 2 FIRE 3 | 2 FIRE 3

064   *All right, now if I... repeat five...*
065   *so if I repeat four, it should do the whole program over again.*

066 11:00 | 2 - 15 | 2 FIRE 3 RPT 4

                            | 2 - 15 | 2 FIRE 3 | 2 - 15 | 2 FIRE 3

067   *Well, I think I figured out what it does.*
068   *EXP: SO HOW DOES IT WORK?*
069   *Ok, when you press the repeat key then the number,*
070   *it comes back that many steps and then starts from there*
071   *and goes up to, uh... it proceeds up to the end of the program*
072   *and then it hits the repeat function again.*
073   *It can't go through it twice.*
074   *......*
075   *EXP: GREAT*

Source: D. Klahr and K. Dunbar, Dual Space Search during Scientific Reasoning (*Cognitive Science, 12,* 1988), p. 13. Copyright 1988 by Ablex Publishing Company. Reprinted with permission.

erated by a subject who very rapidly discovered how *RPT* works.) At the outset, the subject (ML) forms the hypothesis that *RPT N* will repeat the entire program *N* times (003–004). The prediction associated with the first "experiment" is that BigTrak will go forward 6 units (010–011). The prediction is consistent with the current hypothesis, but BigTrak does not behave as expected: it goes forward only 4 units, and the subject comments on the possibility of a failed prediction (013). This leads him to revise his hypothesis: *RPT N* repeats only the last step (019). At this point, we do not have sufficient information to determine whether ML thinks there will be one or *N* repetitions of the last step, and his next experiment (021) does not discriminate between the two possibilities. (We call this kind of hypothesis "partially specified," because of the ambiguity. In contrast, the initial hypothesis stated earlier (003–004) is "fully specified.") However, his subsequent comments (024–025) clarify the issue. The experiment at (021) produces results consistent with the hypothesis that there will be *N* repetitions (BigTrak goes forward 2 units and turns left 60 units), and ML explicitly notes the confirming behavior (022). But the next experiment (026) disconfirms the hypothesis. Although he makes no explicit prediction, we infer from previous statements (023–025) that ML expected BigTrak to go forward 2 and turn left 120. Instead, it executes the entire $\uparrow 2 \leftarrow 30$ sequence twice. ML finds this "strange" (028), and he repeats the experiment.

At this point, based on the results of only four distinct experiments, ML begins to formulate and verbalize the correct hypothesis—that *RPT N* causes BigTrak to execute one repetition of the *N* instructions preceding the *RPT* (030–034)—and he even correctly articulates the special case where *N* exceeds the program length, in which case the entire program is repeated once (035–037). ML then does a series of experiments where he only varies *N* in order to be sure he is correct (038–046), and then he explores the issue of the *order* of execution of the repeated segment. (Klahr and Dunbar, 1988, pp. 12–15)

Klahr and Dunbar (1988) found that their subjects use a wide variety of hypotheses. The researchers employed M. Minsky's concept of frames:

We can think of a frame as a network of modes and relations. The top levels of a frame are fixed, and represent things that are always true about the supposed situation. The lower levels have many *terminals*—slots that must be filled by specific instances or data. Each terminal can specify conditions its assignments must meet. (The assignments themselves are usually smaller subframes.) Simple conditions are specified by *markers* that might require a terminal assignment to be a person, an object of sufficient value, or a pointer to a subframe of a certain type. More complex conditions can specify relations among the things assigned to several terminals. . . . The effects of important actions are mirrored by *transformations* between the frames of a system. These are used to make certain kinds of calculations economical, to represent changes of emphasis and attention, and to account for the effectiveness of imagery. . . . For nonvisual kinds of frames, the differences between the frames of a system can represent actions, cause–effect relations, or changes in conceptual viewpoint. *Different frames of a system share the same terminals;* this is the critical point that makes it possible to coordinate information gathered from different viewpoints. (Minsky, 1981, p. 96)

Subjects' hypotheses were construed as occurring in a hypothesis space, and the frame representation (Minsky, 1975) was used to understand the detailed characteristics of hypotheses that the subjects developed regarding how the *RPT* key functioned.

There are two principle subsidiary frames for *RPT,* N-role:*counter* and N-role:*selector*. . . .

This frame representation is a convenient way of capturing a number of aspects of the scientific reasoning process. First, it characterizes the relative importance that subjects give to different aspects of an hypothesis. Once a particular frame is constructed, the task becomes one of filling in or verifying "slots" in that frame. The current frame will determine the relevant attributes. That is, the choice of a particular role for N (e.g., N-role:*counter*), also determines what slots remain to be filled (e.g., number-of-repetitions: N), and it constrains the focus of experimentation. (Klahr and Dunbar, 1988, pp. 18–19)

Klahr and Dunbar (1988) found that all 20 subjects began with an incorrect statement of how the *RPT* key worked and that, following different strategies, all subjects eventually made the appropriate discovery. There were two main strategies that subjects used in searching for the correct frame: search through the experiment space or search through the hypothesis space. Subjects who used the former discovery strategy were termed "Experimenters," and those who used the latter discovery strategy were termed "Theorists." For all subjects, the pace of discovery was accelerated when the representational frame was changed from N-role:*counter* frame to N-role:*selector* frame. Experimenters and theorists used different strategies in abandoning the N-role:*counter* frame and in choosing the N-role:*selector* frame. These strategies are described below.

Theorists: General Strategy.

The strategy used by the Theorists was to construct an initial frame, N-role:*counter,* and then to conduct experiments that test the values of the frame. When they had gathered enough evidence to reject an hypothesis, theorists switched to a new value of a slot in the frame. For example, a subject might switch from saying that the prior step is repeated N times to saying that the prior program is repeated N times. When a new hypothesis was proposed, it was always in the same frame, and it usually involved a change in only one attribute. . . .

Theorists switched frames by searching memory for information that enabled them to construct a new frame, rather than by further experimentation. Knowing that sometimes the previous program was repeated, the Theorists could infer that the unit of repetition was variable and that this ruled out all hypotheses in the N-role:*counter* frame — these hypotheses all require a fixed unit of repetition. This enabled Theorists to constrain their search for an N-role that permits a variable unit of repetition. As will be shown in Study 2, subjects can construct an N-role:*selector* frame without further experimentation. Following memory search, Theorists constructed the N-role:*selector* frame, and proposed one of the hypotheses within it. They usually selected the correct one, but if they did not, they soon discovered it by changing one attribute of the frame as soon as their initial N-role:*selector* hypothesis was disproved.

Experimenters: General Strategy.

Subjects in the Experimenter group went through two major phases. During the first phase, they explicitly stated the hypothesis under consideration, and conducted experiments to evaluate it. In contrast, during the second phase, they conducted many experiments without any explicit hypotheses. Experimenters used a variety of initial approaches. Some proposed new hypotheses by abstracting from the result of a prior experiment, and they proposed many hypotheses. . . . Others stuck doggedly to the same hypotheses, abandoning them only after much experimentation.

The second phase was an exploration of the experiment space. This can be inferred from the number of experiments conducted without explicit statement of an hypothesis: prior to the discovery of how the repeat works, the Experimenters conducted, on average, 6 experiments without statements of an hypothesis. Furthermore, these experiments were usually accompanied by statements about what would happen if N . . . were changed. By pursuing this approach, the Experimenters eventually conducted an experiment . . . [in which] they noticed that the last N steps were repeated and proposed . . . the correct rule. (Klahr and Dunbar, 1988, pp. 24–25)

The Second Experimental Study of the Discovery Process

The major objective of the second experimental study was to determine whether subjects could propose the function of the *RPT* key without conducting any experiments. The method for the study was as follows:

Subjects. Ten Carnegie Mellon undergraduates participated in the experiment for course credit. Five subjects had taken at least one programming course, and the other five had no programming experience.

Procedure. The familiarization part of Study 2 was the same as described for Study 1; subjects learned how to use all the keys except the *RPT* key. Familiarization was followed by two phases: hypothesis-space search and experimentation.

The hypothesis-space search phase began when the subjects were asked to think of various ways that the *RPT* key might work. In an attempt to get a wide range of possible hypotheses from the subjects, we used three probes in the same fixed order:

1. "How do you think the *RPT* key might work?"
2. "We've done this experiment with many people, and they've proposed a wide variety of hypotheses for how it might work. What do you think they may have proposed?"
3. "When BigTrak was being designed, the designers thought of many different ways it could be made to work. What ways do you think they may have considered?"

After each question, the subject responded with as many hypotheses as could be generated. Then the next probe was used.

Once the subjects had generated all the hypotheses that they could think of, the experimental phase began: The subjects were allowed to conduct experiments while attempting to discover how the *RPT* key works. (Klahr and Dunbar, 1988, p. 28)

The major findings for the hypothesis phase and for the experimental phase were as follows:

Phase 1: Hypothesis-Space Search: Subjects proposed, on average, 4.2 different hypotheses. All but two subjects began with the N-role:*counter* frame, and 7 of the 10 subjects switched to the N-role:*selector* frame during Phase 1. The correct rule . . . was proposed by 5 of the 10 subjects.

Phase 2: Experimentation. All subjects were able to figure out how the RPT key works. . . . [The] mean time to solution was 6.2 minutes, and the subjects generated, on average, 5.7 experiments and proposed 2.4 different hypotheses. (Klahr and Dunbar, 1988, p. 29)

A comparison of Theorists and Experimenters yielded the following results:

In this study, there were six Experimenters and four Theorists. . . . [All] of the Theorists stated the correct rule during the hypothesis-search phase and . . . they all had prior programming experience. (Klahr and Dunbar, 1988, p. 30)

Comparison of Theorists and Experimenters across the two experimental studies disclosed the following interesting differences:

The experiment-space search patterns in this study are radically different from those in Study 1. The Study 2 Experimenters conducted far fewer experiments than either the Experimenters or the Theorists of Study 1. Subjects in Study 2 switch hypotheses more readily; in Study 1, both the Experimenters and the Theorists changed their hypotheses after disconfirmation only 44% of the time. In Study 2 . . . , the Theorists changed hypotheses after disconfirmation 85% of the time and the Experimenters changed after 58%. (Klahr and Dunbar, 1988, p. 30)

Scientific Discovery as Dual Search: The SDDS Model

Klahr and Dunbar (1988) proposed a general model of the processes of scientific discovery, called SDDS (scientific discovery as dual search). The major theme of the model is that of search within and between two spaces: a hypothesis space and an experiment space. Their model developed out of the two experimental studies that were discussed in the previous sections. The major features of the SDDS model are as follows:

SDDS: General Description

We start by summarizing the key features of our model of scientific discovery as dual search (SDDS). It is proposed as a general model of scientific reasoning that can be applied to any context in which hypotheses are proposed and data is collected. The fundamental assumption is that scientific reasoning requires search in two related problem spaces: the hypothesis space, consisting of the hypotheses generated during the discovery process, and the experiment space, consisting of all possible experiments that could be conducted. Search in the hypothesis space is guided both by prior knowledge and by experimental results. Search in the experiment space may be guided by the current hypothesis, and it may be used to generate information to formulate hypotheses.

SDDS consists of a set of basic components that guide search within and between the two problem spaces. Initial hypotheses are constructed by a series of operations that result in the instantiation of a frame with default values. Subsequent hypotheses within that frame are generated by changes in values of particular slots, and changes to new frames are achieved either by a search of memory or by generalizing from experimental outcomes. (Klahr and Dunbar, 1988, p. 32)

The SDDS model contains three major components, described as follows:

SDDS Components. . . . Three main components control the entire process from the initial formulation of hypotheses, through their experimental evaluation, to the decision that there is sufficient evidence to accept an hypothesis. The three components, shown at the top of the hierarchy in [Figure 4.6] are SEARCH HYPOTHESIS SPACE, TEST HYPOTHESIS, and EVALUATE EVIDENCE.

— The output from SEARCH HYPOTHESIS SPACE is a fully specified hypothesis, which provides the input to TEST HYPOTHESIS.

Figure 4.6
Process Hierarchy for SDDS

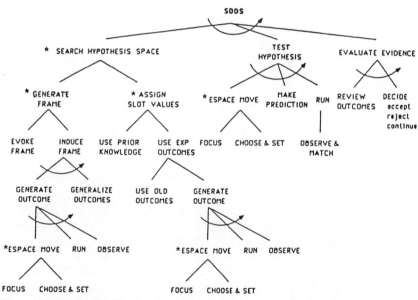

Source: D. Klahr and K. Dunbar, Dual Space Search during Scientific Reasoning (*Cognitive Science, 12,* 1988), p. 14. Copyright 1988 by Ablex Publishing Company. Reprinted with permission.

Note: All subprocesses connected by an arrow are executed in a sequential conjunctive fashion. All process names preceded by an asterisk include conditional tests for which subprocesses to execute.

— TEST HYPOTHESIS generates an experiment appropriate to the current hypothesis (E-SPACE MOVE), makes a prediction, and observes the outcome. The output of TEST HYPOTHESIS is a description of evidence for or against the current hypothesis, based on the match between the prediction derived from the current hypothesis and the actual experimental result.
— EVALUATE EVIDENCE decides whether the cumulative evidence — as well as other considerations — warrants acceptance, rejection, or continued consideration of the current hypothesis.

These processes and their subcomponents are hierarchically depicted in [Figure 4.6], which is described in the following paragraphs. (Klahr and Dunbar, 1988, pp. 32–33)

The search hypothesis space contains two subcomponents, described as follows:

Search hypothesis: Subcomponents. SEARCH HYPOTHESIS SPACE has two components. If there is no active frame, then the system generates one. Usually a new frame has unfilled slots, so the next step is to assign specific values to those slots. If there is an active frame, it may require changes in some slot values.

— GENERATE FRAME has two components corresponding to the two ways that a frame may be generated.
— EVOKE FRAME is a search of memory for information that could be used to construct a frame. This is the process in which the wide variety of prior knowledge sources — discussed earlier — would influence the formation of hypotheses. We will not attempt a detailed elaboration of how specific knowledge elements are activated on the basis of the current context, for that would occupy an entire volume. The main purpose of isolating EVOKE FRAME in SDDS is to distinguish it from the other possible source of new frames: INDUCE FRAME.
— INDUCE FRAME generates a new frame by induction from a series of outcomes.

— The first subprocess in INDUCE FRAME generates an outcome, and the second process generalizes over the results of that (and other) outcomes to produce a frame. GENERATE OUTCOMES will be described below. The specific termination rule and the mechanism for cumulating outcomes are unspecified. The result from GENERATE OUTCOME is a behavior pattern that is input to GENERALIZE OUTCOMES, which then attempts to generalize over the outcomes in order to produce a frame.

The distinction between EVOKE FRAME and INDUCE FRAME corresponds to the difference beween situations in which subjects are able to recall similar situations and use them as the basis for constructing initial frames, and situations in which subjects must observe some behavior before they can venture even an initial hypothesis.

— The purpose of ASSIGN SLOT VALUES is to take a partially instantiated frame and assign specific values to the slots so that a fully specified hypothesis can be generated. It has two components for which we have not specified a preferred order. Values may be assigned by using prior knowledge (USE PRIOR KNOWLEDGE) or by using specific experimental outcomes (USE EXPERIMENTAL OUTCOMES).

  — If there are already some experimental outcomes, then they can be examined to determine specific slot values (USE OLD OUT-COMES).
  — Alternatively, the system can use GENERATE OUTCOME to produce some behavior solely for the purpose of determining slot values.

In the early phases of the discovery process, USE PRIOR KNOWLEDGE plays the major role in assigning values, whereas later in the course of experimentation, USE EXPERIMENTAL OUTCOMES is more likely to generate specific slot values. If the system is unable to assign slot values to the current frame (because they have all been tried and rejected), then the frame is abandoned, and the system returns to GENERATE FRAME. The end result of SEARCH HYPOTHESIS SPACE is a fully specified hypothesis, which is then input to TEST HYPOTHESIS. Note that "experiments" may be run in two different subcontexts in the service of SEARCH HYPOTHE-SIS SPACE, and that neither of these contexts involve the evaluation of an hypothesis, for it is still being formed. (Klahr and Dunbar, 1988, pp. 33, 35)

There are three subcomponents of Test Hypothesis, described as follows:

Test Hypothesis: Subcomponents. TEST HYPOTHESIS uses three subcomponents to: formulate and experiment (E-SPACE MOVE), make a prediction, and run the experiment.

— E-SPACE MOVE produces an experiment. It will be described below, as it is used in several places in the model.
— MAKE PREDICTION takes the current hypothesis and the current experiment and predicts specific results, centered on the current focal values.
— RUN the experiment, OBSERVE the result, and MATCH to expectation. RUN produces a description of a discrepancy between the prediction and the actual behavior. As depicted here, the expected behavior is generated prior to the running of the experiment (during MAKE PREDICTION). However, SDDS allows the computation of what "should have happened" to occur following the running of the experiment, during the MATCH process. MATCH requires descriptions of both the expectation and the observation as input.

TEST HYPOTHESIS outputs a representation of evidence for or against the current hypothesis; this representation is then used as input by EVALU-ATE EXPERIENCE. (Klahr and Dunbar, 1988, p. 35)

In the SDDS model, Evaluate Evidence has the following purposes and functions:

Evaluate Evidence. EVALUATE EVIDENCE determines whether or not the cumulative evidence about the experiments run under the current hypothesis is sufficient to reject or accept it. It is possible that the evidence is inconclusive and neither situation obtains, in which case EVALUATE EVIDENCE loops back to TEST HYPOTHESIS. Note that the input to the review process consists of a cumulation of output from earlier TEST HYPOTHESIS cycles. The scope of this cumulation could range from the most recent result, to the most salient ones, to a full record of all the results thus far. The content of this record could be one of either consistency or inconsistency.

Additional factors may play a role in EVALUATE EVIDENCE. For example, *plausibility* seems to distinguish some of adults' and children's hypotheses, particularly those that perform some arbitrary arithmetic operations on N. *Functionality* arguments appear in some of the protocols, and cause subject to reject hypotheses that have no role to N, even if they have been confirmed (e.g., "why would it take a number if it's not used?", or "why would they design a *RPT* key in the first place?"). Although these factors appear to influence behavior, we do not yet have full understanding of how they work. (Klahr and Dunbar, 1988, p. 36)

The process of Generate Outcomes is briefly described as follows:

Generate Outcome. This process consists of an E-SPACE MOVE, which produces an experiment, RUNning the experiment and OBSERVing the result. (Klahr and Dunbar, 1988, p. 36)

The function of E-Space Move is to design experiments:

E-Space Move. Experiments are designed by E-SPACE MOVE. The most important step is to FOCUS on some aspect of the current situation that the experiment is intended to illuminate. "Current situation" is not just a circumlocution for "current hypothesis," because there may be situations in which there is no current hypothesis, but in which E-SPACE MOVE must function nevertheless. . . . If there is an hypothesis, then FOCUS determines that some aspects of it is the primary reason for the experiment. If there is a frame with open slot values, then FOCUS will select any one of those slots as the most important thing to be resolved if there is neither a frame nor an hypothesis — that is, if E-SPACE MOVE is being called by IN-

DUCE FRAME, then FOCUS makes an arbitrary decision about what aspect of the current situation to focus on.

Once the focal value has been determined, CHOOSE sets a value in the Experiment Space that will provide information relevant to it, and SET determines the values of the remaining, but less important, values necessary to produce a complete experiment. (Klahr and Dunbar, 1988, p. 36)

The storage and retrieval functions of the SDDS model are important, and are described as follows:

Memory Requirements. A variety of memory requirements are implicit in our description of SDDS, and must, by implication, play an important role in the discovery process. Here we provide a brief indication of the kinds of information about experiments, outcomes, hypotheses, and discrepancies that SDDS must store and retrieve.

— Recall that GENERATE OUTCOME operates in two contexts. Under INDUCE FRAME it is called when there is no active hypothesis, and the system is attempting to produce a set of behaviors that can then be analyzed by GENERALIZE OUTCOMES in order to produce a frame. Therefore, SDDS must be able to represent and store one or more experimental outcomes each time it executes INDUCE FRAME.

— Another type of memory demand comes from EVALUATE EVIDENCE: in order to be able to weight the cumulative evidence about the current hypothesis, REVIEW OUTCOMES must have access to the results produced by MATCH in TEST HYPOTHESIS. This would include selected features of experiments, hypotheses, predictions, and outcomes.

— Similar information is accessed whenever ASSIGN SLOT VALUES calls on USE PRIOR KNOWLEDGE or USE OLD OUTCOMES to fill in unassigned slots in a frame.

At this point in the model's development, the precise role of memory remains an area for future research. (Klahr and Dunbar, 1988, pp. 36–37)

Klahr and Dunbar (1988) described the complex interactions of the processes of SDDS as follows:

The Multiple Roles of Experimentation of SDDS. Examination of the relationship among all these processes and subprocesses, depicted in [Figure 4.6], reveals both the conventional and unconventional characteristics of the model. At the top level, the discovery process is characterized as a simple repeating cycle of generating hypotheses, testing hypotheses, and reviewing the outcomes of the test. Below that level, however, we can begin to see the complex interaction among the subprocesses. Of particular importance is the way in which E-SPACE MOVE occurs in three different places in the hierarchy:

1. As a subprocess deep within GENERATE FRAME, where the goal is to generate a behavior pattern over which a frame can be induced,
2. as a subprocess of ASSIGN SLOT VALUES where the purpose of the "experiment" is simply to resolve the unassigned slots in the current frame,
3. as a component of TEST HYPOTHESIS, where the experiment is designed to play its "conventional role" of generating an instance (usually positive) of the current hypothesis.

Note that the implication of the first two uses of E-SPACE MOVE is that in the absence of hypotheses, experiments are generated atheoretically, by moving around in the experiment space.

SDDS also elaborates the details of what can happen during the EVALU-ATE EVIDENCE process. Recall that three general outcomes are possible: The current hypothesis can be accepted, it can be rejected, or it can be considered further.

— In the first case, the discovery process simply stops, and asserts that the current hypothesis is the true state of nature.
— In the second case — rejection — the system returns to H-space search, where two things can happen. If the entire *frame* has been rejected by EVALUATE EVIDENCE, then the model must attempt to generate a new frame. If EVOKE FRAME is unable to generate an alternative frame, then the system will wind up in INDUCE FRAME and will ultimately start to run experiments (in GENERATE OUTCOME) in order to find some element of behavior from which to do the induction. Having induced a new frame, or having returned from EVALUATE EVIDENCE with a frame needing new slot values (i.e., a rejection of the hypothesis but not the frame), SDDS executes ASSIGN SLOT VALUES. Here too, if prior knowledge is inadequate to make slot assignments, the system may wind up making moves in the experiment space in order to make the assignments (i.e., GENERATE OUTCOME under USE EXPERIMENTAL OUTCOMES). In both these cases, the behavior we would observe would be the running of "experiments" without fully-specified hypotheses. This is precisely what we see in the second phase of the Experimenters' behaviors. . . .
— In the third case, SDDS returns to TEST HYPOTHESIS in order to further consider the current hypothesis. The experiments run in this context correspond to the conventional view of the role of experimentation. During MOVE IN E-SPACE, FOCUS selects particular aspects of the current hypothesis and designs an experiment to generate information about it.

(Klahr and Dunbar, 1988, pp. 37–38)

SDDS has the important function of specifying the details and interrelationships among initial knowledge state, knowledge attained from results of experiments, the search through a hypothesis space, and the search through an experiment space. Although SDDS is intended to be a general model, it can, perhaps, best be explicated by application to the two experimental studies described in earlier sections.

Hypothesis Formation and Scientific Discovery. One of the central features of SDDS is that it accounts for two different aspects of hypothesis generation: how hypotheses are generated and why on some occasions there are large differences between adjacent hypotheses, while on others there are only minor differences. Consider first how hypotheses are generated. In SDDS, hypotheses can be generated either from prior knowledge or by generalizing from the results of prior experiments. These two possible knowledge sources play a role both in SEARCH HYPOTHESIS SPACE (EVOKE FRAME and INDUCE FRAME) and in ASSIGN SLOT VALUES (USE PRIOR KNOWLEDGE and USE EXPERIMENTAL OUTCOMES). EVOKE FRAME has its strongest effect at the beginning of the task; subjects formulate their initial hypotheses on the basis of the frame(s) most activated by the features of their current focus. Once subjects have exhausted all the relevant values of a frame, they will again use SEARCH HYPOTHESIS SPACE. Some subjects construct a new frame by using EVOKE FRAME, and others construct it by using the results from INDUCE FRAME.

Differences in the degree of similarity between adjacent hypotheses is a consequence of the use of frames. Initial experimentation is directed at the resolution of particular slot values within a frame. The slot values are changed as a result of prior knowledge (USE PRIOR KNOWLEDGE) or experimentation (USE EXPERIMENTAL OUTCOMES). This leads to the postulation of hypotheses that differ in only minor respects, as subjects change the values only a few at a time. Thus, when subjects search within a frame there will be only minor differences between adjacent hypotheses. When new frames are generated, there will be large differences between hypotheses: recall that when there is a change of frames there is a change in the types of attributes on all the slots, resulting in a radically different knowledge state. . . .

Tolerating Disconfirming Evidence. Recall that our subjects frequently maintained their current hypotheses in the face of negative information. In Study 1, fewer than half of the disconfirming outcomes lead to immediate hypothesis changes. SDDS suggests some possible explanations for this behavior. One contributing factor is the probabilistic nature of the basic processes underlying TEST HYPOTHESIS and EVALUATE EVIDENCE. An unanticipated consequence of the complexity of our procedure was that — due to the fallibility of memory and of the OBSERVE & MATCH processes — the feedback subjects received had some probability of error. That is, from the subjects' perspective, there might be error in either the device behavior, their encoding of that behavior, or their recall of the current program and associated prediction. Gorman (1986) demonstrated that when subjects are told that there is some probability of error in the feedback received during a rule discovery task they tend to "immunize" their hypotheses against disconfirmation by classifying disconfirming instances as the erroneous trials. Thus, some cases of perseveration may result from subjects simply not believing the outcome and attributing the apparent disconfirmation to one of several fallible processes. The most likely candidates for this explanation are the cases in which the subject not only retains a disconfirmed hypothesis, but actually repeats exactly the same experiment. . . . Another error-related cause of perseveration may be even simpler: Subjects erroneously encode the disconfirming behavior as confirming behavior.

The non-deterministic nature of experimental evidence can also have an effect on the decision mechanism in EVALUATE EVIDENCE. This process is based not only on whether the result of the prior experiment rules out the hypothesis, but also on whether enough evidence has accumulated to accept or reject the hypothesis. The amount of evidence in favor of a hypothesis and the strength of the hypothesis both determine when subjects will continue to hold or will switch an hypothesis. Only when the cumulative disconfirming evidence exceeds a criterion will an hypothesis be changed. In the present study, subjects had general sources of prior knowledge that predisposed them to the N-role:*counter* frame. These hypotheses had a high apriori strength and needed much disconfirming evidence to be rejected. However, once the initial hypotheses were rejected, subjects conducted few experiments on subsequent hypotheses. Because these subsequent hypotheses had lower strength, any evidence that appeared to contradict them quickly led to their rejection. Other authors have made similar observations. O'Brien et al., for example, note that "subjects are less likely to take evidence as conclusive when their presuppositions about the content domain discourage them from doing so" (p. 509).

An alternative explanation that has been offered for the finding that subjects tend to stick to disconfirmed hypotheses is that they cannot think of alternative hypotheses. Einhorn and Ogarth (1986), suggest that:

> because the goal of causal inference is to find some explanation for the observed effects, the discounting of an explanation by specific alternatives still leaves one with the question, 'If X did not cause Y, what did?' . . . In fact, the distinction between testing hypotheses and searching for better ones can be likened to the difference between a 'disconfirmation' versus 'replacement' mode of inference. The replacement view is consistent with the Kuhnian notion that theories in science are not discarded, despite evidence to the contrary, if they are not replaced by better alternatives (Kuhn, 1962). Indeed, the replacement view is equally strong in everyday inference. (pp. 14–15)

The results from our studies provide a basis for elaborating this view. We know that when subjects do have alternatives readily available—as in Study 2—they are more likely to drop disconfirmed hypotheses than when they don't—as in Study 1. On the other hand, when subjects could no longer think of any new hypotheses, they could decide to search the experiment space and not hold any hypotheses at all. Thus, subjects did not have to stick with their hypotheses once they had accumulated enough evidence to reject them, because it was permissible in our study to replace something with nothing. (Klahr and Dunbar, 1988, pp. 43-44)

Commentary

The concept of scientific discovery as dual search, represented in the SDDS model, must be examined with respect to two significant and interrelated questions. Does it merely use new terminology for everyday observation or other technical terminologies? Does it explain the key role of insight in scientific discovery?

Traditional explanations of learning and discovery in psychology and everyday explanations have embraced the familiar notions of trial and error: If A doesn't work, try B or C, and if neither of these work, try D, or try for a fresh approach.

Obviously, the interrelationships of search through a hypothesis space and an experiment space and the further details that the SDDS model provides are an analytic advance in the sense of a descriptive advance, but does this microanalysis afford further benefits? A positive answer might be given when it is demonstrated that (a) the SDDS model can be implemented into an actual computer program, and (b) the computer program can model scientific discoveries at a level of complexity beyond that of discovering how an aspect of an electronic device operates.

The problem of insight is explained by Klahr and Dunbar (1988) as simply the replacement of an existing frame with a new frame, which they take to be equivalent to Simon's (1977) equating of insight to finding a new representation for the problem.

Representational change accompanying a new frame can be viewed as a form of illumination or insight (cf. Dunker, 1945; Wallas, 1926). As Simon (1977, p. 333) notes, although research on insight commonly assumes that "asking the right question is the crucial creative act," it is more likely that "reformulation of questions — more generally, modification of representations — is one of the problem-solving processes" and that "new representations, like new problems, do not spring from the brow of Zeus, but emerge by gradual — and very slow — stages."

Our results are consistent with this view. None of our subjects started with the correct general frame. However, once they were driven to it by earlier failed hypotheses and observation of results, they were able to form the correct hypothesis. In other words, results of failed experiments forced subjects to consider the role of N, and this caused a restructuring of the hypothesis space. If restructuring is conceived as generation of a new frame then the nature of insight becomes obvious. Insight is not merely the change of values in slots of a pre-existing frame, rather it is the instantiation of a new frame—this is what is meant by a restructuring of the representation. The interaction between the experiment space and the hypothesis space plays a crucial role in such restructuring. (Klahr and Dunbar, 1988, p. 41)

Both the "new frame" and the "new representation" explanations seem merely descriptive and post-hoc. These explanations grow out of the Gestalt tradition (Ohlsson, 1984a, 1984b) in which a reorganization of the Gestalt (configuration) or the field results in a solution to the problem. Again, this is descriptive and post-hoc.

What needs to be explained is the nature of the mechanism that leads to the "new frame," "new representation," or "new Gestalt." The unconscious processes (Feldman, 1988; Hadamard, 1949; Langley and Jones, 1988; Torrance, 1988) that lead to the small insights of laboratory studies of the discovery process and that lead to great insights of scientific discovery in astronomy, mathematics, biology, and molecular genetics (see section on the general logic of the scientific discovery process in this chapter) remain a scientific enigma whose decipherment may depend on neither psychological laboratory experimentation nor computational models that flow from observations or self-reports of subjects and scientists, but on advances in the neural sciences in conjunction with psychological and computational approaches.

Just as the mind in its many facets stands as the major "general" target for current neurobiological work, creative efforts are among the most important "specifics" in need of elucidation. Numerous electrophysiological and neuroradiological tools now make feasible studies of individual differences. . . .

One other point worth stressing is that neurobiologists can now expect to receive aid from researchers working at the other side of the cognitive-scientific interface. Many psychologists and artificial intelligence researchers working at the level of "domain" or "intelligence" are now probing cognitive processes in great detail; an account in terms of underlying neurophysiological or neurochemical processes is no longer remote. And when it comes to the study of particular human faculties, ranging from language to vision, there is again a cadre of workers prepared to see their work analyzed in terms of underlying biological systems. (Gardner, 1988, p. 318)

A complete science of the nature of scientific discovery processes cannot beg the question of the heart of the discovery process by using different terminologies equivalently limited to only a descriptive function, but rather must possess a theory capable of predicting, under specified conditions, the emergence of new creative insights. The possibility of such a theory remains an inviting and honorable destiny.

FIVE

Language and Representation

In this chapter, the effect of different modes of language representation on the efficiency of information processing is considered. A comparison is drawn between information cast in a sentential representation and the same information cast in a diagrammatic representation. A theory is developed that diagrammatic representation, as compared with sentential representation, possesses greater efficiencies of search and greater efficiencies of recognition. These search and recognition advantages of diagrammatic representation are exemplified by the solution of problems in physics and mathematics.

In the first example, a physics problem (the mechanics of a system of pulleys, weights, and ropes) is initially presented in natural language. The natural language presentation is then given formal representation with respect to the data of the problem and the program (physics knowledge in the form of production rules) necessary to solve the problem. Represented sententially, the process of search for data elements needed by the program is lengthy and cumbersome. Represented diagrammatically, data elements are grouped together at a single location, and the search is more efficient.

In the second example, a problem in plain geometry is first given in natural language. The natural language is then transformed into sentential and diagrammatic representations. The sentential representation of lines, angles, and points of intersection requires an extensive list of labelled elements. In contrast, the diagrammatic representation of the same information results in simple and efficient recognition of elements and relationships at given locations.

In a commentary it is pointed out that, although diagrammatic representations may possess search and recognition advantages in applied problem solving, they may create difficulties for advances in abstract conceptualization. A discussion of how dependence on geometric representation has created difficulties for conceptual development in certain areas of theoretical mathematics concludes the chapter.

LANGUAGE REPRESENTATION MODES AND INFORMATION-PROCESSING EFFICIENCY

Language and the Representation of Reality

Language serves to epitomize, consolidate, regularize, and, generally, to simplify by its various modes of representation the diffuse and myriad events of the world of physical reality and the phenomenological world of personal reality. Diffuse personal emotions can be given representation as concrete visual images in painting and sculpture, epitomized in musical expression or poetic metaphor, or captured in epigrammatic formulations. Diverse physical phenomena can be regularized as principles of motion or energy, and can be given representation in lucid and powerful equations such as the standard wave equation which has uniform application to the physics of sound, light, electricity, and magnetism, or in the spectrum of wavelengths which as a diagrammatic representation can capture, depict, and interrelate the essential characteristics of what would otherwise be the chaos of electromagnetic and chemical phenomena.

The result of all these varieties of language representation is a vast improvement in the efficiency and immediacy of comprehension. A diagram, a map, or a picture can greatly reduce the effort needed to comprehend the same information when in a textual or sentential form. In the present section, I shall describe and comment on the research of J. H. Larkin and H. A. Simon (1987) as presented in their article "Why a Diagram Is (Sometimes) Worth Ten Thousand Words."

Formal Representation of Diagrams and Sentences

Information — its amount and its processing — can be construed as independent of its biological or electronic locus. The representation of information in a general information-processing system, human or

computer, can take a variety of modes that entail differential consequences for the efficiency of information processing. In order to understand why differential modes of representation entail differential
computational efficiencies, it is useful to construe them in a common
formal language that can facilitate their comparison and contrast.
Larkin and Simon (1987) developed a formal analysis for comparing
the relative computational efficiencies of diagrammatic and sentential representations of the same information.

> To understand why it is advantageous to use diagrams — and when it is — we
> must find some way to contrast diagrammatic and non-diagrammatic repre-
> sentations in an information-processing system. . . .
>   We consider external problem representations of two kinds, both of which
> use a set of symbolic expressions to define the problem.
>
> 1. In a *sentential* representation, the expressions form a sequence correspond-
>   ing, on a one-to-one basis, to the sentences in a natural-language descrip-
>   tion of the problem. Each expression is a direct translation into a simple
>   formal language of the corresponding natural language sentence.
> 2. In a *diagrammatic* representation, the expressions correspond, on a one-to-
>   one basis, to the components of a diagram describing the problem. Each
>   expression contains the information that is stored at one particular locus in
>   the diagram, including information about relations with the adjacent loci.
>
> The fundamental difference between our diagrammatic and sentential repre-
> sentations is that the diagrammatic representation preserves explicitly the
> information about the topological and geometric relations among the com-
> ponents of the problem, while the sentential representation does not. A sen-
> tential representation may, of course, preserve other kinds of relations, for
> example, temporal or logical sequence. An outline may reflect hierarchical
> relations. (Larkin and Simon, 1987, pp. 65–66)

To compare two representations in a general way, it is useful to
begin with the question of their essential isomorphism. For example,
in mathematics, an algebraic representation and a geometric representation are isomorphic in the system of analytic geometry, where
correspondents and mutual derivation exist for equations and curves.
Larkin and Simon (1987) defined the conditions under which two
representations possess informational and computational equiva-
lents:

> At the core of our analysis lie the wholly distinct concepts of *informa-*
> *tional* and *computational* equivalence of representations (Simon, 1978). Two
> representations are informationally equivalent if all of the information in

the one is also inferable from the other, and vice versa. Each could be constructed from the information in the other. Two representations are computationally equivalent if they are informationally equivalent and, in addition, any inference that can be drawn easily and quickly from the information given explicitly in the one can also be drawn easily and quickly from the information given explicitly in the other, and vice versa.

"Easily" and "quickly" are not precise terms. The ease and rapidity of inference depends upon what operators are available for modifying and augmenting data structures, and upon the speed of these operators. When we compare two representations for computational equivalence, we need to compare both data and operators. The respective value of sentences and diagrams depends on how these are organized into data structures and on the nature of the processes that operate upon them. (Larkin and Simon, 1987, p. 67)

The efficiency of a computational system can be construed as a function of the interrelationships among and quality of fitness between search, recognition, and inference processes operating on a specific representation of information. Sentential representation and diagrammatic representation may have differential consequences for the operations of search, recognition, and inference:

Search. Consider . . . the sentential data structure consisting of a simple list of items. Unless an index is manufactured and added explicitly to this list, finding elements matching the conditions of any inference rule requires searching linearly down the data structure. Furthermore, the several elements needed to match conditions for any given rule may be widely separated in the list. Search times in such a system depend sensitively upon the size of the data structure.

Search in a diagram can be quite different. In this representation an item has a location. If the conditions of an inference rule are only satisfied by structures at or near a single location, then the tests for satisfaction can all be performed on the limited set of structures that belong to the current location, and no search is required through the remaining data. Often part of the search process involves identifying multiple attributes of the same items, for example, that a rabbit is both white and furry. Therefore one computational cost of search is the ease with which such attributes can be collected. . . .

The two systems just described are not, in general, computationally equivalent. As we have described them, we would expect the second to exhibit efficiencies in search that would be absent from the first. Differences in search strategies associated with different representations are one major source of computational inequivalence.

Recognition. The effects of different representations on search are at least equaled by their effects on recognition. Human abilities to recognize information are highly sensitive to the exact form (representation) in which the information is presented to the senses (or to memory). For example, consider a set of points presented either in a table of x and y coordinates or as geometric points on a graph. Visual entities such as smooth curves, maxima and discontinuities are readily recognized in the latter representation, but not in the former.

Ease of recognition may be strongly affected by what information is explicit in a representation, and what is only implicit. For example, a geometry problem may state that a pair of parallel lines is cut by a transversal. Eight angles, four exterior and four interior, are thereby created but not mentioned explicitly. Moreover, without drawing a diagram it is not easy to identify which pairs of angles are alternate interior angles — information that may be needed to match the conditions of an inference rule. All of these entities are readily identified from a diagram by simple processes, once the three lines are drawn. The process of drawing the diagram makes these new inferences which are then displayed explicitly in the diagram itself. . . . Of course, the same information can also be inferred from the sentential representation, but these latter inference processes may require substantial computation, and the cost of this computation must be included in any assessment of the relative efficiency of the two representations. . . .

Inference. In view of the dramatic effects that alternative representations may produce on search and recognition processes, it may seem surprising that the differential effects on inference appear to be less strong. Inference is largely independent of representation *if* the information content of the two sets of inference rules is equivalent — i.e., the two sets are isomorphs as they are in our examples. But it is certainly possible to make inference rules that are more or less powerful, independently of representation. (Larkin and Simon, 1987, pp. 69–71)

Comparison of Representations: First Example

Data Structure and Program

The differential computational efficiency of sentential representation and diagrammatic representation can be demonstrated by analysis of a problem in elementary mechanics. The problem illustrates, in particular, the differential effects of the two representations on the efficiency of search. The problem is first presented in ordinary natural language as it might appear in a physics textbook. The natural language text is then transformed into two formal representations, sentential and diagrammatic, and the representations are then compared with respect to efficiency of search processes.

The Given Data Structure and Program

Consider a problem given in the following natural language statements. We have three pulleys, two weights, and some ropes, arranged as follows:

1. The first weight is suspended from the left end of a rope over Pulley A. The right end of this rope is attached to, and partially supports, the second weight.
2. Pulley A is suspended from the left end of a rope that runs over Pulley B, and under Pulley C. Pulley B is suspended from the ceiling. The right end of the rope that runs under Pulley C is attached to the ceiling.
3. Pulley C is attached to the second weight, supporting it jointly with the right end of the first rope.

The pulleys and ropes are weightless; the pulleys are frictionless; and the rope segments are all vertical, except where they run over or under the pulley wheels. Find the ratio of the second to the first weight, if the system is in equilibrium. . . .

We formalize and simplify the natural language sentences in this problem to produce the elements listed in [Table 5.1, section (a)]. The labels 1a, 1b, and so forth, refer to the sentence numbers above, with the decimal numbers labeling successively elements produced from a single sentence.

The first propositions in each sentence associate labels with appropriate objects. We read subsequent propositions, for example, (1a.1) as: the weight W1 is suspended from the rope Rp. We read proposition (1a.2) as: The rope, consisting of the left-hand segment Rp and the right-hand segment Rq, runs over (or under) the wheel of pulley Pa. Sentences 2 through 3 are similarly translated. At the end, we add element (4.1) giving a specific simple value to the weight W1 which can then be related to the value of weight W2 in order to answer the question. We have captured the original problem statement, accurately we believe, in these formal elements that use the relations of *hangs, pulley-system,* and *value.*

In this data structure the various object labels (e.g., W1, Rx) are essential. It is only through these labels that one can infer that two different elements (e.g., 1b.1 and 3b.3) both refer to the weight W2. In the original problem statement these connections were provided (somewhat obscurely) by a combination of labels and anaphoric, numeric, and locational references (e.g., "supporting it jointly with the right end of the first rope"). (Larkin and Simon, 1987, pp. 72–73)

Having transformed the natural language statement of the problem into a corresponding data structure as depicted in Table 5.1a, inference procedures based on principles of physics are then applied to the data structure to attain a solution to the problem. The inferential procedures take the form of production rules (if–then, condition–action):

Table 5.1

Formal Data Structure (a) and Program (b) for the Pulley Problem

(a)

(Weight W1) (Rope Rp) (Rope Rq) (Pulley Pa)
(1a.1)   (hangs W1 from Rp)
(1a.2)   (pulley-system Rp Pa Rq)

(Weight W2)
(1b.1)   (hangs W2 from Rq)

(Rope Rx) (Pulley Pb) (Rope Ry) (Pulley Pc) (Rope Rz)
(Rope Rt) (Rope Rs) (Ceiling c)
(2a.1)   (hangs Pa from Rx)
(2a.2)   (pulley-system Rx Pb Ry)
(2a.3)   (pulley-system Ry Pc Rz)
(2b.1)   (hangs Pb from Rt)
(2b.2)   (hangs Rt from c)

(3a.1)   (hangs Rx from c)
(3a.2)   (hangs Rs from Pc)
(3a.3)   (hangs W2 from Rs)

(4a.1)   (value W1 1)

(b)

P1. *Single-string support.* (weight <Wx>) (rope <ry>)
   (value <Wx> <n>) (hangs <Wx> <Ry>)
   -(hangs <Wx> <Rx>)
   - (value <Ry> <W-number>)

P2. *Ropes over pulley.* (pulley <P>) (rope <R1>) (rope <R2>)
   (pulley-system <R1> <P> <R2>) (value <R1> <n1>)
   - (value <R2> <n1>)

P3. *Rope hangs from or supports pulley.* (pulley <R1>) (rope <R1>) (rope <R2>)
   (pulley-system <R1> <P> <R2>) { (hangs <R3> from <P>) or (hangs <P>
   from <R3>) } (value <R1> <n1>) (value <R2> <n2>)
   - (value <R3> <n1> + <n2>)

P4. *Weight and multiple supporting ropes.* (weight <W1>) (rope <R1>) (rope
   <R2>) (hangs <W1> <R1>) (hangs <W1> <R2>) ~(hangs <W1> <R3>)
   (value <R1> <n1>) (value <R2> <n2>)
   - (value <W1> <n1> + <n2>)

Source: J. H. Larkin and H. A. Simon, Why a Diagram Is (Sometimes) Worth Ten Thousand
   Words (*Cognitive Science, 11,* 1987), p. 74.

We now turn from the given data structure to the program, composed of
physics knowledge, that will act on it to solve the problem. This program
consists of the following inference (or production) rules based on a few principles of statics. Pointed brackets (⟨ ⟩) indicate variables that refer to particular objects (e.g., ropes, pulleys).

P1. *Single-string support.* Given a weight of known value ⟨n⟩ and a rope ⟨R⟩ from which it hangs, if there is no other rope from which it hangs (indicated by the symbol ∿), then the supporting rope also has value (tension) ⟨n⟩ associated with it.

P2. *Ropes over pulley.* If a pulley system ⟨P⟩ has two ropes ⟨R1⟩ and ⟨R2⟩ over it, and the value (tension) associated with ⟨R1⟩ is ⟨n1⟩, then ⟨n1⟩ is also the value associated with rope ⟨R1⟩.

P3. *Rope hangs from or supports pulley.* If there is a pulley system with ropes ⟨R1⟩ and ⟨R2⟩ over it, and the pulley system hangs from a rope ⟨R3⟩, and ⟨R1⟩ and ⟨R2⟩ have the values (tensions) ⟨n1⟩ and ⟨n2⟩ associated with them, then the value (tension) associated with ⟨R3⟩ is the sum of ⟨n1⟩ plus ⟨n2⟩.

P4. *Weight and multiple supporting ropes.* If a weight ⟨W1⟩ hangs from both ropes ⟨R1⟩ and ⟨R2⟩, but hangs from no other ropes, and the values ⟨n1⟩ and ⟨n2⟩ are associated with ⟨R1⟩ and ⟨R2⟩, then the value associated with ⟨W1⟩ is the sum of ⟨n1⟩ plus ⟨n2⟩.

[Table 5.1, section (b)] shows these rules, stated then in a formal notation matching that used for the data structure in [Table 5.1, section (a)]. In this notation symbols with pointed brackets can be matched to any symbol. A "∿" indicates an element that may not appear in the current data structure if the conditions of the rule are to be satisfied.

These inference rules are based on two physics principles. (1) The total force on an object at rest is zero. (2) The tensions are equal in all parts of an ideal (massless, frictionless) rope, even if this rope passes over ideal (massless, frictionless) pulleys. The productions are directions for applying these principles in several specific situations relevant to our problem. Principles must be rewritten as active inference rules for any problem solving system. (Indeed, students may well be unable to solve problems in part because they learn principles, and do *not* translate them into inference rules.) (Larkin and Simon, 1987, pp. 73–75)

Sentential Representation for the First Example

The pulley problem, originally given in natural language, and subsequently represented as a data structure (Table 5.1, section (a)) can be solved by application of the program (Table 5.1, section (b)). The solution steps reveal the encumbering effects on search processes and memory load that result from a sentential representation:

Using the program in [Table 5.1, section (b)], the problem can be solved by a simple non-algebraic procedure. Applying our physics inference rules, we develop sequentially values associated with objects in the problem, ultimately finding the desired value associated with weight W2. In English, the steps of this solution are:

Table 5.2
Solution to the Pulley Problem Using the Sentential Representation

Original Element	Productions	P1	P2	P3	P2	P2	P3	P4
	Steps	1	2	3	4		5	6
1. (Weight W1)		x	o	o	o			o
(Rope Rp)		x	x	x	o			o
(Rope Rq)		o	x	x	o			x
(Pulley Pa)		o	x	x	o			o
(hangs W1 from Rp)		x	o	o	o			o
(pulley-system Rp Pa Rq)		o	x	x	o		o	o
(Weight W2)		o		o	o	o	o	x
(hangs W2 from Rq)		o		o	o	o	o	x
2. (Rope Rx)		o		x	x	o	o	o
(Pulley Pb)		o		o	x	o	o	o
(Rope Ry)		o		o	x	x	x	o
(Pulley Pc)		o		o	o	x	x	o
(Rope Rz)		o		o	o	x	x	o
(Rope Rt)		o		o	o	o	o	o
(Rope Rs)		o		o	o	o	o	o
(Ceiling c)		o		o	o	o	x	x
(hangs Pa from Rx)		o		x	o	o	o	o
(pulley-system Rx Pb Ry)		o			x	o	o	o
(pulley-system Ry Pc Rz)		o				x	x	o
(hangs Pb from Rt)		o					o	o
(hangs Rt from c)		o					o	o
3. (hangs Rz from c)		o					o	o
(hangs Rs from Pc)		o					x	o
(hangs W2 from Rs)		o					o	x
(value W1 1)		x					o	o
New Elements								
(value Rp 1)		x	x				x	
(value Rq 1)			x				o	
(value Ry 2)				x			o	
(value Rx 2)					x	x	o	
(value Rz 2)						x	o	
(value Rs 4)							x	
(value W2 5)								o

Total Elements Searched: 138

	25	7	20	19	14	22	31

Source: J. H. Larkin and H. A. Simon, Why a Diagram Is (Sometimes) Worth Ten Thousand Words (*Cognitive Science, 11,* 1987), p. 77.

1. Because weight W1 (value 1) hangs from rope Rp and no other rope, the value associated with Rp is 1.
2. Because Rp (value 1) and Rq pass over the same pulley, the value of Rq is 1.
3. Because Rp and Rq have values 1, and the pulley Pa over which they pass is supported by Rx, the value associated with Rx is $1 + 1 = 2$.
4. Because Rx (value 2) and Ry pass over the same pulley, the value of Ry is 2.

5. Because Ry (value 2) and Rz pass under the same pulley, the value of Rz is 2.
6. Because Ry and Rz have values 2, and the pulley Pc under which they pass is supported by Rs, the value associated with Rs is $2 + 2 = 4$.
7. Because weight W2 is supported by rope Rq (value 1) and rope Rs (value 4) and by no other ropes, its value is $1 + 4 = 5$.

(Larkin and Simon, 1987, pp. 75–76)

The seven solution steps can be processed using the formal representation of the elements and the application of inference (or production) rules to the elements, as depicted in Table 5.2:

[Table 5.2] shows the seven steps of the solution using the formal representation developed earlier. The original elements of the data structure are listed at the left, and the seven steps, with the production applied, across the top. At the bottom are the new elements added to the data structure in that step. In each column, an x indicates an element that must be present for the inference rule to apply, and an o indicates an element that must be searched (assuming the simple linear search strategy outlined above) in order to verify that the production applies.

In step 1, for example, rule P1, *Single-string support,* is matched by the four x'd elements to conclude that the value associated with rope segment Rp is 1. All other elements must also be searched, however, to assure that weight W1 is not supported by any rope other than Rp, one of the conditions of this inference rule. This kind of difficulty arises in using any inference rule based on finding all instances of a particular class, and examples in physics are common. (The net force is the sum of *all* forces acting on the system; energy is conserved if there are *no* dissipative processes.) (Larkin and Simon, 1987, pp. 76–77)

Diagrammatic Representation for the First Example

Where the logic of the sentential representation exacted heavy costs in search and memory, the logic of diagrammatic representation results in efficient search and computation because information elements are at one location or, at most, at adjacent locations. Figure 5.1 depicts the configuration of locations of information relevant to the solution of the pulley problem. In Figure 5.1, lines connect adjacent locations, and the focus of search is confined to a single location or to an adjacent location.

Table 5.3 shows the data structure and locations for the pulley problem. The solution is produced by application of inference rules:

Figure 5.1
Schematic Diagram of Locations in the Diagrammatic Representation

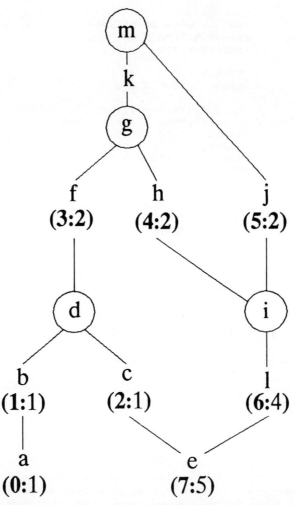

Source: J. H. Larkin and H. A. Simon, Why a Diagram Is (Sometimes) Worth Ten Thousand
    Words (*Cognitive Science, 11,* 1987), p. 79. Copyright 1987 by Ablex Publishing Com-
    pany. Reprinted with permission.
Note: "Adjacent" locations are connected (see text). Steps in the solution are shown
    in bold, with the value added to the location following the relevant step.

Based on this data structure, and using the same physics program as before,
the solution to the pulley problem is as follows:

1. A weight at a, with associated value 1, hangs from something at b, which is
   a rope. Therefore the rope at b has associated value 1. (*Single-string sup-*
   port, No search, Attention now at b.)

Table 5.3
Data Structure for the Pulley Problem (with locations indicated by lowercase labels a, b, c)

	(Weight a)(Rope b)(Rope c)(Pulley d)
(1a.1)	(hangs a from b)
(1a.2)	(pulley-system b d c)
	(Weight e)
(1b.1)	(hangs e from c)
	(Rope f)(Pulley g)(Rope h)(Pulley i)(Rope j)
	(Rope k)(Rope l)(Ceiling m)
(2a.1)	(hangs d from f)
(2a.2)	(pulley-system f g h)
(2a.3)	(pulley-system h i j)
(2b.1)	(hangs g from k)
(2b.2)	(hangs k from m)
(3a.1)	(hangs j from m)
(3a.2)	(hangs l from i)
(3b)	(hangs e from l)
(4.1)	(value a 1)

Source: J. H. Larkin and H. A. Simon, Why a Diagram Is (Sometimes) Worth Ten Thousand Words (*Cognitive Science, 11,* 1987), p. 78.

2. The rope at b is in the pulley-system at d which also contains the thing at c which is a rope. Therefore the rope at c has associated value 1. (*Ropes over pulley.* Possible to make false attempt to apply *Rope hangs from or supports pulley* to (b c d f). Will fail because value at c is unknown. Attention now at c.)
3. The rope at c (value 1) is in the pulley-system at d which hangs from the things at f which is a rope. The pulley-system at d also contains the things at b which is a rope with value 1. Therefore the value associated with the rope at f is 2. (*Rope hangs from or supports pulley.* Possible alternative step: Apply *Weight and multiple supporting ropes* to (c e 1). Will fail because value at 1 is unknown. Attention now at f.)
4. The rope at f (value 2) is the pulley system at g which also contains the thing at h which is a rope. Therefore the value associated with the thing at h is 2. (*Ropes over pulley.* Attention now at h.)
5. The rope at h is in the pulley-system at i which also contains the thing at j which is a rope. Therefore the value associated with the rope at j is 2. (*Ropes over pulley.* Possible alternative step: Apply *Rope hangs from or supports pulley* to (h i j). Fails because value at j is unknown. Attention now at j.)
6. The rope at j (value 2) is in the pulley-system at i which also contains the thing at h (a rope, value 2) and suspends the thing at l which is also a rope. Therefore the value associated with rope l is 4. (Rope hangs from or supports pulley. No search alternatives. Attention at l.)
7. The thing at l (a rope, value 4) suspends the thing at e which is a weight,

also suspended from the thing at c which is a rope with associated value 1. Therefore the value of the weight at e is 5. (*Weight and multiple supporting ropes.* No search alternatives. Attention at e.)

(Larkin and Simon 1987, pp. 79–80)

Summary

Computational efficiency results from the substitution of the language of diagrams for the language of words as demonstrated in the analysis of solutions processes for the pulley problem.

We assume that change of attention to an adjacent location is a computationally easy process. Therefore, the searches and inferences indicated above comprise essentially all of the work of solving this problem. . . . Compared with the 138 considerations of elements for the sentential representation (see [Table 5.2]), the diagrammatic representation provides a large saving.

Note also that the object labels in the sentential data structure (e.g., W1, PA) have been replaced by locations. Thus in addition to cutting search, a diagrammatic representation eliminates the overhead of keeping track of object labels. (Larkin and Simon, 1987, p. 80)

Comparison of Representations: Second Example

The Given Representation of the Problem

The geometry problem and the knowledge needed to solve it are first presented in natural language. The problem (data structure) and the knowledge (program) are then construed as sentential and diagrammatic representations. The two representations are then compared in computational efficiency with respect to search, labelling, and recognition processes.

The given problem representation consists, as stated below, of a verbal statement of the problem (the given data structure), together with textbook statements of the definitions and axioms needed to solve the problem (the given program).

1. Two transversals intersect two parallel lines and intersect with each other at a point x between the two parallel lines.
2. One of the transversals bisects the segment of the other that is between the two parallel lines.
3. Prove that the two triangles formed by the transversals are congruent. . . .

The given program consists of the following axioms and theorems from geometry.

P1. *Definition of Bisector.* If something is a bisector, then it divides a line segment into two congruent segments.

P2. *Alternate Interior Angles.* If two angles are alternate interior angles, then they are congruent.

P3. *Vertical Angles.* If two angles are vertical angles then they are congruent.

P4. *ASA.* If two angles and the included side of one triangle are congruent to the corresponding two angles and included side of another triangle, then the triangles are congruent.

(Larkin and Simon, 1987, pp. 82–83)

Sentential Representation for the Second Example

In Table 5.4, the natural language of the geometry problem has been replaced with a formal data structure. The complexities of search and recognition processes for the sentential representation are clear and significant:

Even with a data structure adequate for recognition, *search* is still problematic. If we imagine a sentential representation consisting of the list of elements in [Table 5.4], then to match each element in an inference rule, we must search through the entire list until we find it, an average of $48/2 = 24$ tests.

In short, in this simple geometry problem, recognition of the conditions for an inference rule, and search for matching conditions are both significant problems in a sentential representation. (Larkin and Simon, 1987, p. 90)

Diagrammatic Representation for the Second Example

The natural language statement of the problem can be easily transformed into a diagram such as that of Figure 5.2. From that diagram, the configural arrangement of parallel lines and transversals, interior and exterior angles, triangles, point of intersection, and so forth, is readily discerned. In order to reason about these configurations and to reach a proof as required by the problem, the inference rules of Table 5.5 can be applied.

How can we take the data structure in [Table 5.4] and the program in [Table 5.5] and interpret it as a diagrammatic representation? As in the case of the pulley problem, let us assume that we have a perceptual control mechanism that allows the system to have instant access to all information at a given location; specifically, we assume that if two elements refer to the same point, then they are at the same location. The spacing in [Table 5.5] groups together (for the first three rules) elements at a single location. For these rules,

Table 5.4
Elements in the Final Perceptually Enhanced Data Structure (including (a) original elements, (b) elements added by perceptual productions, and (c) elements added by the geometry program)

(a)

(parallel lines 4 and 5)
(transversal 6 of 4 and 5)
(transversal 7 of 4 and 5)
(intersect 6 and 7 in x)
(between x lines 4 5)
(segment 16 of 6)
(segment 16 between 4 and 5)
(bisector 7 of 6)

(b)

(point x on lines 6 and 7)
(point 14 on lines 6 and 4)
(point 15 on lines 6 and 5)
(segment 16 from 14 to 15)
(point x on segment 16)
(segment 18 joining x and 15)
(segment 19 joining x and 14)
(point 20 on lines 5 and 7)
(segment 21 joining 20 and x)
(segment 22 joining 20 and 15)
(point 23 on 4 and 7)
(segment 24 joining 23 and 20)
(point x on segment 24)
(x is between 20 and 23)
(segment 26 joining 23 and x)
(segment 27 joining 23 and 14)
(point 23 in line 6 region 1)
(point 20 in line 6 region 2)
(point 23 in line 5 region 1)
(point 14 in line 5 region 1)
(point x in line 5 region 1)
(point 20 in line 4 region 1)
(point 15 in line 4 region 1)
(point x in line 4 region 1)
(point 15 in line 7 region 1)
(point 14 in line 7 region 2)
(angle 38: vertex 14 line 6 region 1 line 4 region 1)
(angle 39: vertex x line 7 region 2 line 6 region 1)
(angle 40: vertex 23 line 7 region 2 line 4 region 1)
(triangle 41 is: 23 x 14)
(segment 27 is in triangle 41)
(segment 26 is in triangle 41)

Table 5.4 (continued)

(segment 19 is in triangle 41)
(angle 42: vertex 15 line 6 region 2 line 5 region 1)
(angle 43: vertex x 7 line 1 region 6 line 2 region)
(angle 44: vertex 20 line 7 region 1 line 5 region 1)
(triangle 45 is: 20 x 15)
(segment 22 is in triangle 45)
(segment 21 is in triangle 45)
(segment 18 is in triangle 45)

(c)

(alternate interior angles 44 40
 angle vertex 20 line 7 region 1 line 5 region 1
 angle vertex 23 line 7 region 2 line 4 region 1)
(vertical angles 39 43
 vertex x line 6 region 1 line 7 region 2
 vertex x line 6 region 2 line 7 region 1)
(alternate interior angles 42 38
 angle vertex 15 line 6 region 2 line 5 region 1
 angle vertex 14 line 6 region 1 line 4 region 1)
(segments 15 x and 14 x are congruent
 definition of bisector)
(congruent triangles
 segments 15 x and 14 x
 angles vertex 15 line 5 region 1 line vertex 14 line 4 region 1
 angles vertex x line 6 region 2 vertex x line 6 region 1)

Source: J. H. Larkin and H. A. Simon, Why a Diagram Is (Sometimes) Worth Ten Thousand Words (*Cognitive Science, 11,* 1987), p. 86. Copyright 1987 by Ablex Publishing Company. Reprinted with permission.

information is always present at just one or two locations. If we make the primitive assumption that there is no guidance for locating the first object in a group, then search will be required through an average of $(48/2) = 24$ elements. But thereafter no further search is required for any elements in a location group. The number of elements that must be checked to satisfy a production referring to n locations is therefore n* $(48/2)$, assuming also that each group is found independently of the last. In contrast, the number of elements checked in the sentential representation is N* $(48/2)$ where N is the number of elements in the production. Therefore the grouping of about 10 elements per production in [Table 5.5] into one or two location groups reflects the search advantage of a diagrammatic representation. The fourth rule (ASA) contains two location groups, each corresponding to one triangle, and each related to three point locations joined by segments. The rule is written to emphasize the pairs of congruent parts, rather than the locations. By our criterion that "same location" means "contains a common point," this rule covers four locations in two adjacent pairs. Furthermore, the points

Figure 5.2
Diagram for the Geometry Problem (Labels Correspond to Table 5.4)

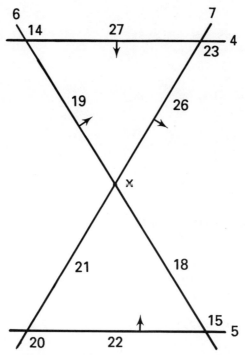

Source: J. H. Larkin and H. A. Simon, Why a Diagram Is (Sometimes) Worth Ten Thousand Words (*Cognitive Science, 11,* 1987), p. 83. Copyright 1987 by Ablex Publishing Company. Reprinted with permission.

in the two locations are related in perceptually predictable ways (although this organization is not captured by our formal representation).

These estimates of relative search difficulty are extremely conservative. If a person can search for two or three things simultaneously, one search can find the conditions of a production with spatial groupings. Furthermore, two separate location groups in a production are often at predictably related locations (e.g., at opposite ends of a transversal). (Larkin and Simon, 1987, p. 92)

Summary

As shown by the above analysis, the diagrammatic representation, as compared with the sentential representation, confers computational efficiency both with respect to recognition or perceptual aspects of the geometry problem and with respect to search processes.

Table 5.5
Formal Geometry Program in Terms of Primitive Elements (points, lines, and segments)

```
(p bisector
    (bisector by <b> segment <s>)                          ;original condition
     ;<s> bisected by <b>

    (line<b>)                                              ;definition of bisector
    (point <p> on <b>)
     ;line <b> with <p> on it

    (segment <s>)
    (point <p> on <s>)
     ;segment <s> with <p> on it

    (segment <s> endpoints <p1> <p2>)
     ;endpoints of <s>
    (segment <s1> endpoints <p1> <p>)
    (segment <s2> endpoints <p2> <p>)
     ;subsegments of <s> formed by <p>

    - (congruent <s1> <s2>)
     ;this inference has already been made

    (congruent <s1> <s2>)

(p vertical
    (angle <a1> vertex <v> line <l1> region <n1>
                            line <l2> region <n2>)
    (angle { <a2> <> <a1> } vertex <v>
                line <l1> region { <n3> <> <n1> }
                line <l2> region { <n3> <> <n1> })
    - (congruent object <a1> <a2>)

    (make congruent> objects <a1> <a2>))
```

Source: J. H. Larkin and H. A. Simon, Why a Diagram Is (Sometimes) Worth Ten Thousand Words (*Cognitive Science, 11,* 1987), p. 89–90. Copyright 1987 by Ablex Publishing Company. Reprinted with permission.

The major difference in a diagrammatic representation, we believe, is difference in recognition processes. We have seen that formally producing perceptual elements does most of the work of solving the geometry problem. But we have a mechanism—the eye and the diagram—that produces exactly these "perceptual" results with little effort. We believe the right assumption is that diagrams and the human visual system provide, at essentially zero cost, all of the inferences we have called "perceptual." As shown above, this is a huge benefit. If the geometry problem is given verbally, without a diagram, all of these elements must be constructed explicitly (or perhaps in part by some internal imaging process). It is exactly because a diagram "produces" all the elements "for free" that it is so useful.

In this problem, as in the pulley problem, using a diagram removed the need for labelling the objects. Because there are so many objects in the geometry problem, this is a considerable saving. In the formal OPS5 system, all objects are defined in terms of points, that is, in terms of their locations. Informally, it is common to construct a geometry proof simply by making corresponding congruent elements in a diagram that need not include any labels at all. The labels are needed only when a conventional proof is written — and that is, in fact, a sentential representation. . . .

Although in the geometry problem there are large differences in the recognition and search processes required by the sentential and diagrammatic representations, there are no differences in inference processes. In each case four geometric inferences are required to solve the problem. (Larkin and Simon, 1987, pp. 92-93)

Commentary

Larkin and Simon (1987) have clarified the role of diagrams in the solution of certain types of problems as they occur in physics or geometry. As compared with words, diagrams possess locational and recognitional advantages.

However, I should like to point out that the relationship between diagrams and words is important because representation relates to thought. In the remainder of this section, I will comment on diagrammatic representation as resulting sometimes in the facilitation of thought and sometimes in its hindrance.

Diagrams and Metaphorical Thought

Diagrams can be considered as perceptual metaphors that function as a language of the concrete to render abstraction palpable. Thus, Darwin in *The Origin of Species* ([1872] 1936) relied on the diagram of the "Tree of Life" as a metaphor for his theory of evolution, wherein the concepts of death and survival of certain lines of species and biological forms could be given perceptual representation.

During the modification of the descendants of any one species, and during the incessant struggle of all species to increase in numbers, the more diversified the descendants become, the better will be their chance of success in the battle for life. Thus the small differences distinguishing varieties of the same species, steadily tend to increase, till they equal the greater differences between species. . . .

The green and budding twigs may represent existing species; and those produced during former years may represent the long succession of extinct species. . . . *The Tree of Life.* . . . fills with its dead and broken branches the crust of the earth, and covers the surface with its ever-branching and beautiful ramifications. (Darwin, [1872] 1936, pp. 99–100, italics added)

Diagrams and Mathematical Thought

Although diagrams are usually considered as facilitating thought, the reliance on diagrams can also be seen to inhibit thought. Thus, the development of mathematical thought was blocked for many centuries by the reliance on geometric diagrams as a test for the existence of mathematical concepts. Two examples are the concepts of higher-degree equations and infinite or transfinite numbers.

The Greeks were able to solve quadratic equations and cubic equations by giving them representations as geometric diagrams. Even the terms *quadratic* and *cubic* reveal geometric representation and geometric solution of equations. Equations of higher degree, such as quartic equations, possess no geometric representation and were essentially ignored by the Greeks. In subsequent centuries, the replacement of geometric diagrams and geometric thought by analytic notation and analytic thought permitted the development of a theory of solution for equations of the nth degree (Kline, 1980).

Greek mathematical thought represented numbers geometrically, as a diagram of a line of points. The actuality of numbers depended on the reality of physical representation. The actuality of infinite numbers could not be represented as an actual line of points. Greek mathematical thought thereby excluded infinite numbers and, indeed, it was only with the relinquishment of geometric representation (numbers construed as finite lengths of lines) that the central concepts of modern mathematical infinity and infinitesimals and their conceptualization in symbolic logic could be developed (Robinson, 1966).

SIX

Conclusion

In this book, we have been concerned with problems of the intellectual range and level of artificial intelligence and human cognition. The intellectual range has been broad: from a comparison of mathematical proof by mathematicians and by computers, to a comparison of legal reasoning by human jurisprudence and computer jurisprudence; from the nature of rationality in mathematical models of economic behavior to the nature of rationality in probabilistic models of psychological judgment; from the rationality of simple mathematical description to the rationality of theoretical mathematical analysis; from an analysis of computational approaches to problem solving in the natural sciences to an analysis of problem solving in medical diagnosis; and from a computer modelling of scientific discovery processes in biochemistry to a computational analysis and comparison of sentential and diagrammatic representation in information processing systems.

The most impressive intellectual achievements of artificial intelligence, considered in this book, are, in order of rank: (1) that a computer could make highly essential intellectual contributions to the proof of a mathematical theorem whose establishment had eluded the maximal efforts of human mathematicians for a century, (2) that a computer could intellectually outperform Harvard Law School students in the detection of legal issues contained in a problem in contract law, (3) that a computer could replicate the complex processes of scientific discovery used by an outstanding and original biochemist, and (4) that a computer could use the general intellectual principles of decomposition and invariance to solve problems in specific domains of physical science.

Beyond these intellectual achievements that artificial intelligence has attained, a number of goals that still beckon were discussed in the book: (1) the prospect of using the computer as an intellectual partner in the establishment of mathematical proofs that require highly intricate, complex, and lengthy deductive processes, (2) the provision of deeper knowledge and multiple frames of reference in case law that would enable computer jurisprudence to model more closely the wisdom level of human jurisprudence, (3) to provide to the computer an advanced conceptual facility with which to more closely model the level of human cognition characteristic of theoretical science, and (4) to provide the computer with an increased capacity for the flexible representation of problems that would permit a closer modelling of the adaptive ingenuity found in human problem solving.

At the beginning of this book, I quoted Herbert Simon's prediction that the ability of computers to think, learn, and create will increase rapidly until, in the visible future, the range of problems they can handle will be coextensive with the range to which the human mind has been applied. Indeed, as discussed in this book, the intellectual ability of the computer has increased in power and in scope, but its *coextensivity* with problems to which the human mind has been applied is still in the visible future. Moreover, the human mind is continuously extending its intellectual range and depth, and its accomplishments do not remain fixed. It is clear that intellectual advancement will characterize both the realm of human intelligence and the realm of artificial intelligence and that a cooperative and synergistic relationship between the realms will culminate in greater advancement than could be achieved by the separate endeavors of either.

Bibliography

American Law Institute. (1932). *Restatement of the Law of Contracts.* 2 vols. St. Paul: American Law Institute Publishers.

American Law Institute. (1981). *Restatement of the Law, Second: Contracts 2d.* 3 vols. St. Paul: American Law Institute Publishers.

Anderson J. R. (1983). *The Architecture of Cognition.* Cambridge, MA: Harvard University Press.

Anderson, J. R. (1985). *Cognitive Psychology and Its Implications* (2nd ed.). New York: W. H. Freeman and Company.

Appel, Kenneth, and Haken, Wolfgang. (1977). Every Planar Map Is Four Colorable, Part I: Discharging. *Illinois Journal of Mathematics, 21,* 429–490.

Appel, Kenneth, and Haken, Wolfgang. (1979). The Four-Color Problem. In L. A. Steen (ed.), *Mathematics Today: Twelve Informal Essays* (pp. 153–180). New York: Springer-Verlag.

Baldwin, E. (1947). *Dynamic Aspects of Biochemistry.* New York: Macmillan.

Beebe, M. (1986, June 22). The Birdman of Jamestown. *Buffalo Magazine,* pp. 10–16.

Berkeley, G. ([1734] 1929). *Essays, Principles, Dialogues, with Selections from Other Writings.* M. W. Calkins (ed.). New York: Charles Scribner.

Bolzano, B. (1950). *Paradoxes of the Infinite.* D. A. Steele (ed.). London: Routledge and Kegan Paul.

Bowne, G. D. (1966). *The Philosophy of Logic, 1880–1908.* The Hague: Mouton.

Boyer, C. B. (1968). *A History of Mathematics.* New York: John Wiley and Sons.

Brownston, L., Farrell, R., Kant, E., and Martin, N. (1985). *Programming Expert Systems in OPS5: An Introduction to Rule-Base Programming.* Reading, MA: Addison-Wesley.

Buchanan, B. G. (1982). New Research on Expert Systems. In J. E. Hayes, Donald Michie, and Y.-H. Pao (eds.), *Machine Intelligence 10.* New York: Halsted Press, John Wiley.

Buchanan, B. G., and Feigenbaum, E. A. (1978). Dendral and Meta-Dendral: Their Application Dimension. *Artificial Intelligence, 11,* 5-24.

Chase, W. G., and Simon, H. A. (1973). Perception in Chess. *Cognitive Psychology, 1,* 35-81.

Crowe, M. J. (1975). Ten "Laws" Concerning Patterns of Change in the History of Mathematics. *Historia Mathematica, 2,* 161-166.

Curry, H. B. (1951). *Outlines of a Formalist Philosophy of Mathematics.* Amsterdam: North Holland.

Darwin, C. ([1872] 1936). *The Origin of Species by Means of Natural Selection* (6th ed.). New York: Modern Library.

Davis, M. (1965). *Applied Nonstandard Analysis.* New York: John Wiley and Sons.

Davis, P., and Hersh, R. (1981). *The Mathematical Experience.* Boston: Birkhauser Boston Inc.

Davis, R., and Lenat, D. (1980). *Knowledge-Based Systems in Artificial Intelligence.* New York: McGraw Hill.

Dieudonne, J. (1971). Modern Axiomatic Methods and the Foundations of Mathematics. In Francois Le Lionnais (ed.), *Great Currents of Mathematical Thought* (Vol. 2, pp. 251-266). New York: Dover.

Duncker, K. (1945). On problem solving. *Psychological Monographs, 58*(5), Whole No. 270.

Einhorn, H. J., and Hogarth, R. M. (1986). Judging probable cause. *Psychological Bulletin, 99,* 3-19.

Einstein, A. (1933). *The Method of Theoretical Physics.* Oxford: Oxford University Press.

Feigenbaum, E. A. (1977a). The Art of Artificial Intelligence: I. Themes and Case Studies of Knowledge Engineering. *Proceedings, Fifth International Joint Conference on Artificial Intelligence.* Cambridge, MA, pp. 1014-1029.

Feigenbaum, E. A. (1977b, August). *The Art of Artificial Intelligence: Themes and Case Studies of Knowledge Engineering.* Stanford Heuristic Programming Project, Memo HPP-77-25. Palo Alto, CA: Stanford University Press.

Feigenbaum, E. A., Buchanan, E. A., and Lederberg, J. (1987). On Generality and Problem Solving: A Case Study Using the DENDRAL Program. In D. Michie (ed.), *Machine Intelligence 6.* Edinburgh, Scotland: Edinburgh University Press, pp. 165–190.

Feldman, D. H. (1988). Creativity: Dreams, Insights, and Transformations. In R. J. Sternberg (ed.), *The Nature of Creativity.* Cambridge: Cambridge University Press, pp. 271–297.

Ferris, T. (1988). *Coming of Age in the Milky Way.* New York: William Morrow and Company, Inc.

Fraenkel, A. A. (1947). The Recent Controversies about the Foundations of Mathematics. *Scripta Mathematica, 13,* 17–36.

Frank, J. (1949). *Courts on Trial: Myth and Reality in American Justice.* Princeton: Princeton University Press.

Freudenthal, H. (1961). *The Concept and Role of the Model in Mathematics and Social Sciences.* Dordrecht: Reidel.

Friedman, M. (1962). *Price Theory.* Chicago, Aldine.

Fruton, J. S. (1972). *Molecules and Life: Historical Essays on the Interplay of Chemistry and Biology.* New York: Wiley-Interscience.

Gardner, A. (1987). *An Artificial Intelligence Approach to Legal Reasoning.* Cambridge, MA: The MIT Press.

Gardner, H. (1988). Creative Lives and Creative Works: A Synthetic Scientific Approach. In R. J. Sternberg (ed.), *The Nature of Creativity.* Cambridge: Cambridge University Press, pp. 298–324.

Gödel, K. (1931). Über formal unentscheidbare Satz de Principia Mathematica und verwandter System, I. *Monatshefte für Mathematica und Physics, 13,* 173–189.

Gödel, K. (1964). What is Cantor's Continuum Problem? In P. Benacerraf and H. Putnam (eds.), *Philosophy of Mathematics, Selected Readings* (pp. 258–273). Englewood Cliffs, NJ: Prentice-Hall.

Golos, E. B. (1968). *Foundations of Euclidean and Non-Euclidean Geometry.* New York: Holt, Rinehart & Winston.

Gorman, M. E. (1986). How the Possibility of Error Affects Falsification on a Task That Models Scientific Problem Solving. *British Journal of Psychology, 77,* 85–96.

Greenberg, M. J. (1974). *Euclidean and Non-Euclidean Geometries: Development and History.* San Francisco: W. H. Freeman.

Grimson, E. W., and Patil, R. S. (eds.). (1987). *AI in the Nineteen Eighties and Beyond: An MIT Survey.* Cambridge, MA: MIT Press.

Gruber, H. E., and Davis, S. N. (1988). Inching Our Way up to Mount Olympus: The Evolving-Systems Approach to Creative Thinking. In R. J. Sternberg (ed.), *The Nature of Creativity.* Cambridge: Cambridge University Press, pp. 243–270.

Guggenheimer, H. (1977). The Axioms of Betweenness in Euclid. *Dialectica, 31,* 187–192.

Hadamard, J. (1949). *The Psychology of Invention in the Mathematical Field.* Princeton, NJ: Princeton University Press.

Hardy, G. H. (1929). Mathematical Proof. *Mind, 38,* 1–25.

Hardy, G. H. (1967). *A Mathematician's Apology.* Cambridge: Cambridge University Press.

Heath, T. L. (1956). *Euclid's Elements* (Vol. 1). New York: Dover.

Hennessey, B. A., and Amabile, T. M. (1988). The Conditions of Creativity. In R. J. Sternberg (ed.), *The Nature of Creativity.* Cambridge: Cambridge University Press.

Hilbert, D. (1964). On the Infinite. In P. Benacerraf & H. Putnam (eds.), *Philosophy of Mathematics: Selected Readings* (pp. 134–151). Englewood Cliffs, NJ: Prentice-Hall.

Holmes, F. L. (1980). Hans Krebs and the Discovery of the Ornithine Cycle. *Federation Proceedings, 39,* 216–225.

Hunt, E. (1989). Cognitive Science: Definition, Status, and Questions. In M. R. Rosenzweig and L. W. Porter (eds.), *Annual Review of Psychology, 40,* 603–629.

Iliev, L. (1972). Mathematics as the Science of Models. *Russian Mathematical Surveys, 27,* 181–189.

John-Steiner, V. (1985). *Notebooks of the Mind.* Albuquerque: University of New Mexico Press.

Kahneman, D., Slovic, P., and Tversky, A. (1982). *Judgment under Uncertainty: Heuristics and Biases.* New York: Cambridge University Press.

Kahneman, D., and Tversky, A. (1982). The Psychology of Preferences. *Scientific American, 246,* 160–174.

Kahneman, D., and Tversky, A. (1984). Choices, Values, and Frames. *American Psychologist, 39,* 341–350.

Kepler, J. (1937). De Motibus Stellae Martis. In *Johannes Kepler Gesammelte Werks.* Munchen: Ch Beck.

Klahr, D., and Dunbar, K. (1988). Dual Space Search during Scientific Reasoning. *Cognitive Science, 12,* 1–48.

Kline, M. (1980). *Mathematics: The Loss of Certainty.* Oxford: Oxford University Press.

Kolata, G. Bari (1976). Mathematical Proof: The Genesis of Reasonable Doubt. *Science, 192,* 989–990.

Korner, S. (1967). On the Relevance of Post-Godelian Mathematics to Philosophy. In I. Lakator (ed.), *Problems in the Philosophy of Mathematics* (pp. 118–133). Amsterdam: North-Holland.

Kuhn, T. S. (1962). *The Structure of Scientific Revolutions.* Chicago: University of Chicago Press.

Kuhn, T. S. (1970). Logic of Discovery or Psychology of research? In I. Lakatos and A. Musgrave (eds.), *Criticism and the Growth of Knowledge, 4.* Cambridge: Cambridge University Press, pp. 126–141.

Kulkarni, D., and Simon, H. A. (1988). The Processes of Scientific Discovery: The Strategy of Experimentation. *Cognitive Science, 12,* 139–175.

Kuttner, Robert (1985, February). The Poverty of Economics. *The Atlantic Monthly,* pp. 74–84.

Lakatos, I. (1976). *Proofs and Refutations.* J. Worral and E. Zaher (eds.). Cambridge: Cambridge University.

Langley, P. (1981). Data-Driven Discovery of Physical Laws. *Cognitive Science, 5,* 31–54.

Langley, P., and Jones, R. (1988). A Computational Model of Scientific Insight. In R. J. Sternberg (ed.), *The Nature of Creativity.* Cambridge: Cambridge University Press, pp. 177–201.

Langley, P., Simon, H., A., Bradshaw, G. L., and Zytkow, J. (1987). *Scientific Discovery: Computational Explorations of the Creative Processes.* Cambridge, MA: MIT Press.

Larkin, J., McDermott, J., Simon, O. P., and Simon, H. A. (1980). Expert and Novice Performance in Solving Physics Problems. *Science, 208,* 1335–1342.

Larkin, J. H., Reif, F., Carbonell, J., and Gugliotta, A. (1988). FERMI: A Flexible Expert Reasoner with Multi-Domain Inferencing. *Cognitive Science, 12,* 101–138.

Larkin, J. H., and Simon, H. A. (1987). Why a Diagram Is (Sometimes) Worth Ten Thousand Words. *Cognitive Science, 11,* 65–99.

Lehninger, A. L. (1982). *Principles of Biochemistry.* New York: Worth Publishers.

Lenat, D. (1977). On Automated Scientific Theory Formation: A Case Study Using the AM Program. In J. E. Hayes, D. Michie, and L. Mikulich (eds.), *Machine Intelligence 9.* New York: Halstead Press, pp. 251–286.

Leontief, W. (1982, July). Academic Economics (letter). *Science, 217,* 104, 107.

Lindley D. V., Tversky, A., and Brown, R. V. (1979). On the Reconciliation of Probability Assessments. *Journal of the Royal Statistical Society, 142,* 146–180.

Luck, J. M. (1932). *Annual Review of Biochemistry.* Stanford, CA: Stanford University Press.

Mackie, G. L. (1973). *Truth, Probability, and Paradox.* New York: Oxford University Press.

McCorduck, P. (1979). *Machines Who Think.* San Francisco: W. H. Freeman.

Mehrtens, Herbert. (1976). T. S. Kuhn's Theories and Mathematics. *Historia Mathematica, 3,* 297–320.

Merlan, P. (1960). *From Platonism to Neoplatonism.* The Hague: Martinus Nijoff.

Minsky, M. (1975). A Framework for Representing Knowledge. In P. H. Winston (ed.), *The Psychology of Computer Vision*. New York: McGraw-Hill, pp. 211-217.

Minsky, M. (1981). A Framework for Representing Knowledge. In J. Haugeland (ed.), *Mind Design*. Cambridge, MA: MIT Press, pp. 95-128.

Newell, A., Shaw, J. C., and Simon, H. A. (1960). Report on General Problem-Solving Program for a Computer. *Information Processing and Proceedings of the International Conference of Information Processing,* 256-264.

Newell, A., and Simon, H. A. (1972). *Human Problem Solving.* Englewood cliffs, NJ: Prentice-Hall.

Nilsson, N. J. (1980). *Principles of Artificial Intelligence.* Palo Alto, CA: Tioga.

Ohlsson, S. (1984). Restructuring Revisited: An Information Processing Theory of Restructuring and Insight. *Scandinavian Journal of Psychology, 25,* 65-78, 117-129.

Patel, V. L., and Groen, G. J. (1986). Knowledge Based Solution Strategies in Medical Reasoning. *Cognitive Science, 10,* 91-116.

Poincare, H. (1913). *Foundations of Science.* G. B. Halstead (trans.). New York: Science Press.

Polya, G. (1962). *Mathematical Discovery.* New York: John Wiley and Sons.

Post, E. L. (1943). Formal Reductions of the General Combinatorial Decision Problem. *American Journal of Mathematics, 65,* 197-268.

Prenowitz, W., and Jordan, M. (1965). *Basic Concepts of Geometry.* New York: Cambridge University Press.

Rabin, Michael O. (1977). Probabilistic Algorithms. In J. F. Traub (ed.), *Algorithms and Complexity: New Directions and Recent Results.* New York: Academic Press.

Rich, Elaine. (1983). *Artificial Intelligence.* New York: McGraw-Hill.

Robinson, A. (1964). Formalism 64. *Proceedings, International Congress for Logic, Methodology and Philosophy of Science,* pp. 228-246.

Robinson, A. (1966). *Nonstandard Analysis.* Amsterdam: North Holland.

Robinson, A. (1969). From a Formalist's Point of View. *Dialectica, 23,* 45-49.

Rolston, D. (1988). *Principles of Artificial Intelligence and Expert Systems Development.* New York: McGraw-Hill.

Ross, S. L. (1964). *Differential Equations.* New York: Blaisdell.

Russell, B. (1948). *Human Knowledge, Its Scope and Its Limits.* New York: Simon and Schuster.

Russell, B. (1967). *The Autobiography of Bertrand Russell.* Boston: Little, Brown.

Russell, B., and Whitehead, A. N. (1910). *Principia Mathematica.* Cambridge: Cambridge University Press.

Sampson, R. V. (1956). *Progress in the Age of Reason: The Seventeenth Century to the Present Day.* Cambridge: Harvard University Press.

Shafer, G., and Tversky, A. (1983). *Weighing Evidence: The Design and Comparisons of Probability Thought Experiments.* Unpublished manuscript, Stanford University.

Shortliffe, E. (1976). *Computer Based Medical Consultations: MYCIN.* New York: Elsevier.

Simon, H. A. (1977). *Models of Discovery.* Dordrecht, Holland: D. Reidel

Simon, H. A. (1978). On the forms of mental representation. In C. W. Savage, (ed.), *Minnesota Studies in the Philosophy of Science: Vol. 9. Perception and Cognition: Issues in the Foundations of Psychology.* Minneapolis: University of Minnesota Press, pp. 3–18.

Simon, H. A. (1979). Quoted in McCorduck, *Machines Who Think.* San Francisco: W. H. Freeman.

Simon, H. A., and Lea, G. (1974). Problem Solving and Rule Induction: A Unified View. In L. Gregg (ed.), *Knowledge and Cognition.* Hillsdale, NJ: Erlbaum, pp. 105–128.

Smith, Adam. ([1776] 1985). *The Wealth of Nations* (rev. ed.). New York: McGraw Hill.

Steen, L. A. (ed.). (1979). *Mathematics Today: Twelve Informal Essays.* New York: Springer-Verlag.

Sternberg, R. J. (ed.). (1988). *The Nature of Creativity.* Cambridge: Cambridge University Press.

Stroyan, K. D., and Luxemberg, W. A. U. (1976). *Introduction to the Theory of Infinitesimals.* New York: Academic Press.

Torrance, P. E. (1988). The Nature of Creativity as Manifest in Its Testing. In R. J. Sternberg (ed.), *The Nature of Creativity.* Cambridge: Cambridge University Press, pp. 43–75.

Tucker, John (1970, February). *Rules, Automata and Mathematics.* London: The Aristotelian Society.

Tversky, A., and Kahneman, D. (1977). Causal Thinking in Judgment under Uncertainty. In R. Butts and J. Hintikka (eds.), *Basic Problems in Methodology and Linguistics, 3.* Dordrecht: Reidel, pp. 167–192.

Tversky, A., and Kahneman, D. (1983, October). Extensional versus Intuitive Reasoning: The Conjunction Fallacy in Probability Judgment. *Psychological Review, 90,* 293–315.

Tymoczko, Thomas. (1979). The Four-Color Problem and its Philosophical Significance. *Journal of Philosophy, 76,* 57–83.

Tymoczko, Thomas. (1980). Computers, Proofs, and Mathematicians: A Philosophical Investigation of the Four-Color Proof. *Mathematics Magazine, 3,* pp. 131–138.

Wagman, M. (1978). The Comparative Effects of Didactic Correction and Self-Contradiction on Fallacious Scientific and Personal Reasoning.

Journal of General Psychology, 99, 67–80.

Wagman, M. (1980). PLATO DCS, an Interactive Computer System for Personal Counseling. *Journal of Counseling Psychology, 27,* 16–30.

Wagman, M. (1983). A Factor Analytic Study of the Psychological Implications of the Computer for the Individual and Society. *Behavior Research Methods and Instrumentation, 15,* 413–419.

Wagman, M. (1984a). *The Dilemma and the Computer: Theory, Research, and Applications to Counseling Psychology.* New York: Praeger.

Wagman, M. (1984b). Using Computers in Personal Counseling. *Journal of Counseling and Development, 63,* 172–176.

Wagman, M. (1988). *Computer Psychotherapy Systems Theory and Research Foundations.* New York: Gordon and Breach Science Publishers.

Wagman, M. (in press). *Cognitive Science and Concepts of Mind: Toward a General Theory of Human and Artificial Intelligence.*

Wagman, M., and Kerber, K. W. (1980). PLATO DCS, an Interactive Computer System for Personal Counseling: Further Development and Evaluation. *Journal of Counseling Psychology, 27,* 31–39.

Wagman, M., and Kerber, K. W. (1984). Computer-Assisted Counseling: Problems and Prospects. *Counselor Education and Supervision, 24,* 147–154.

Wallas, G. (1926). *The Art of Thought.* New York: Harcourt Brace.

Watson, J. (1968). *The Double Helix: A Personal Account of the Discovery of the Structure of DNA.* New York: Kingsport Press, Inc.

Wechsler, Judith (ed.). (1978). *On Aesthetics in Science.* Cambridge, MA: MIT Press.

Weissinger, Johannes. (1969). The Characteristic Features of Mathematical Thought. In T. L. Saaty and F. J. Weyl (eds.), *The Spirit and Uses of the Mathematical Sciences* (pp. 9–27). New York: McGraw-Hill.

Wilder, Raymond L. (1944). The Nature of Mathematical Proof. *American Mathematical Monthly, 51,* 309–323.

Winograd, T. (1972). *Understanding Natural Language.* New York: Academic.

Zippin, L. (1962). *Uses of Infinity.* Washington, DC: Mathematical Association of America.

Author Index

Subject Index

ABOUT THE AUTHOR

MORTON WAGMAN is Professor Emeritus of Psychology at the University of Illinois, Urbana-Champaign. Professor Wagman is a Diplomate in Counseling Psychology, American Board of Professional Psychology.

Dr. Wagman is the originator of the PLATO computer-based Dilemma Counseling System. PLATO DCS, published by Control Data Corporation, has been internationally used at colleges and universities for research, service, and instructional purposes.

Dr. Wagman's research on computer counseling has been published widely in scientific and professional journals. Professor Wagman's most recent books are *Computer Psychotherapy Systems: Theory and Research Foundations* (1988) and *The Dilemma and the Computer: Theory, Research, and Applications to Counseling Psychology* (Praeger, 1984).

Dr. Wagman was graduated Phi Beta Kappa from Columbia University with honors and special distinction in mathematics. Dr. Wagman holds an M.A. and a Ph.D. in psychology from the University of Michigan.

Professor Wagman has held faculty positions in the departments of psychology at the University of Michigan and at the University of Illinois, where he has also been a clinical counselor. Dr. Wagman is a member of the American Psychological Association and the American Association for the Advancement of Science.